Food Production Technology

Syuzanna Xolmurotova Ismoil qizi

© Syuzanna Xolmurotova Ismoil qizi
Food Production Technology
by: Syuzanna Xolmurotova Ismoil qizi
Edition: July '2024
Publisher:
Taemeer Publications LLC (Michigan, USA / Hyderabad, India)

ISBN 978-93-5872-703-6

© **Syuzanna Xolmurotova Ismoil qizi**

Book	:	Food Production Technology
Author	:	Syuzanna Xolmurotova Ismoil qizi
Publisher	:	Taemeer Publications
Year	:	'2024
Pages	:	160
Title Design	:	*Taemeer Web Design*

BASIC AND RAW MATERIALS OF FOOD PRODUCTION. SCIENTIFIC BASIS OF FOOD PRODUCT TECHNOLOGY

One of the most important tasks of the government of the republic is to meet the growing demand of the population for consumer goods, that is, food. For example, as a result of full supply of food and non-food products to the population, the foundation is created for them to live a prosperous life. Meeting this demand is solved by increasing the number of food enterprises and expanding the base of food raw materials, as well as their rational use, introducing new innovative technologies to the enterprises of the network.

All branches of agricultural products processing enterprises :

As a result of mutual harmonization (integration) and specialization, it is necessary to produce products that satisfy two different needs of the population and deliver them to consumers. The first of them is food production. It forms a complex of food products. It includes bread and bakery products, confectionery, sugar, meat and meat products, tea, grape wine, cognac, vodka, various canned goods and other products. These food products provide the necessary substances for the human body and ensure its healthy growth. At the same time, the agro-industrial complex produces goods that are used in the process of living for the population.

It forms a complex of consumer goods. Footwear, clothing, gas, industrial alcohol, technical oils and other products are produced there. With the development of this complex, the living conditions of the population will change. Here, it is necessary to take into account the provision of the population with other necessary items, tools, as well as housing, various services, etc. it also depends on food safety. Because the volume of production of food products at the national level should ensure the country's need for it without depending on external factors (foreign countries). As a result, political-economic and social stability will be ensured at the country level. During the time when the Republic of Uzbekistan was part of the former union, its demand for flour and flour products was mainly met by products brought to the republic from abroad. It was completely inappropriate to maintain this situation during the independence of the republic. That is why the government of the republic consistently implemented the policy of grain independence from the first years of the transition period. To achieve this, an effort was made to reduce the production volume of raw cotton, which was considered efficient. As a result, the cultivation of potatoes, considered the "second bread", was also developed. Currently, this type of product is not being bought from abroad, for example, state security is being achieved in this regard, but currently the level of supply of meat and meat products, milk and milk products, and fat products to the population of the republic is medical. is much lower than the norm. In order to solve this problem, special attention is paid to the intensive development of all branches of agriculture, which are considered the central link of the agro-industrial complex. Efforts are being made to develop livestock industries at a priority pace. In particular, it is necessary to develop poultry farming on an industrial basis is given importance. All-round economic opportunities are being created for non-state enterprises involved in cattle and sheep breeding. In order to sustainably provide them with financial resources, preferential loans and taxes are being introduced privileges are given, and the tools necessary for their production, imported from abroad, are exempted from customs duties. All these are activities aimed at increasing the amount of consumer goods.

Experts say that 70% of a person's health and longevity depends on his diet and lifestyle, 20% on the state of medical care, and 10% on his vital congenital indicators. The given information gives a clear picture of the importance of food and the industry that produces it in the state of human health and prolonging life.

Food products are necessary for the active and healthy life of the population

Guaranteed physical and economic ability to purchase the amount is the main condition for its survival, social stability of society and positive demographic situation in the country. Currently, the average daily consumption of food products in the EU countries is 3390 kcal, in the USA - 3650, in Latin America - 2790, in developing Asia - 2650 kcal. The average daily food ration in

Uzbekistan is 2700-2800 kcal. Increasing the caloric level of daily food is primarily related to the development of the country's economy and the improvement of people's well-being.

Grains, sugar, beets, tea, coffee, various plant roots, sunflowers, tobacco, potatoes, cotton, vegetables, fruits and other materials obtained from plant science are the main raw materials for the food industry. and other livestock products. Auxiliary materials are cocktail products, and production processes are carried out

helps increase, but is not directly part of the tire product. They are divided into two groups:

a) auxiliary materials used in obtaining the finished product;

b) auxiliary materials consumed by cocktail equipment.

Semi-finished products are raw materials that have been pre-processed and require further processing.

For example, grapes (in their natural state) are semi-finished products for the production of wine, brandy, and alcohol. For example, sugar is a finished product for sugar factories, semi-finished products for refineries and raw materials for confectionery factories. All raw materials produced in the food industry are divided into three groups according to their chemical properties and characteristics:

1. Sectors that process primary agricultural raw materials (sugar beet, oil producing, viticulture, starch-molasses and alcohol producing factories).

2. Sectors using agricultural raw materials whose raw materials have undergone initial processing and are engaged in repeated production (bakeries, confectionery, pasta, refining, beer brewing).

3. Industries that mine and prepare table salt, as well as produce mineral water. The composition of food products is different. Such a diverse product determined by the amount of ingredients. Food raw materials contain substances such as carbohydrates, fats, water, and sugars.

Carbohydrates. Carbohydrates make up most of the dry matter of fruits and vegetables (90%). The average daily ration of an elderly person should consist of 500 g of digestible carbohydrates. Fruit and vegetable carbohydrates include sugars, starch, cellulose, hemicelluloses, and pectin substances. Sugars. Fruits and vegetables contain mainly monosaccharides (hexoses), glucose, fructose and sucrose from disaccharides. There are small amounts of monosaccharides such as arabinose, xylose, mannose, galactose, ribose, rhamnose, sorbose, and disaccharides such as maltose, gensiobiose, and six-atom alcohols (mannitol, sorbitol) similar in structure to sugars. In the human body, glucose and fructose are absorbed directly into the blood. Therefore, they are quickly and well digested. Sucrose is hydrolyzed by the invertase enzyme present in the body, resulting in glucose and fructose. Sugars are distinguished by their sweet taste. The threshold of sweetness (minimum concentration at which a sweet taste is noticeable) is 0.25% for fructose, 0.55% for glucose, and 0.38% for sucrose. Taste indicators depend not only on the amount of sugar in fruits and vegetables, but also on acid, starting substances, essential oils and other compounds. To evaluate the taste indicators of fruits and vegetables, their sugar-acid indicators are found. The sugar-acid index is the ratio of the percentage of sugar to the percentage of acid. The amount of sugar in fruits is on average 8-14%, in grapes it is much more (18-22, sometimes up to 26%). Seed products contain more fructose than sugars, less glucose and sucrose. Cherries, cherries and plums, grapes and other berries are rich in glucose, and sucrose is almost absent. Apricots and peaches have a lot of sucrose, and much less monosaccharides. Vegetables contain an average of 4% sugars. Root fruits (beets, carrots), especially sugar crops (watermelon, melon) have a lot of sugar. Tomatoes, eggplant, peppers, cauliflower, carrots contain more glucose and fructose, and green peas contain more sucrose. The properties of sugars and their changes during processing have a great impact on the choice of technological mode and the quality of the finished product. Sugars are well soluble in water, especially in hot water. Sugars can be lost when fruits and vegetables are washed, if their skins are damaged. When fruits and vegetables are blanched, the sugar content changes. Sugars have hygroscopic properties. This mainly applies to fructose. Considering this, it is not recommended to store non-hermetically sealed canned products (jam, povidlo, dried fruit) in warehouses with high humidity. Sugars are exposed to microorganisms in conditions of sufficient humidity. It is mainly affected by mold and mildew. They develop dramatically at room temperature. Therefore, fruits, vegetables and products made from them should be protected from the effects of microorganisms. Also, fermentation of sugars forms the basis of some technological processes in the processing of plant raw materials (in the preparation of pickles). Starch. Starch is quickly broken down in the human body by an enzymatic way: first, it is hydrolyzed under the action of amylase, broken down into dextrin, then maltose is formed, which, in turn, is broken down into glucose under the action of maltase enzyme. Starch is collected mainly in nuts and grains. Potatoes (12-25%), green peas and sweet corn contain a lot of starch. Many fruits and vegetables are low in starch (around 1%). Food industry enterprises are divided into two large groups according to the type of processed product:

1. Enterprises processing plant raw materials.

2. Enterprises processing animal raw materials.

Plant raw material processing enterprises are divided into primary raw material processing and secondary raw material processing industries. Primary processing enterprises of raw materials can include flour-cereal, powdered sugar, canning, primary winemaking, primary preparation of alcohol, tobacco and tea leaves, vegetable oil production enterprises. Their raw materials are grain, fruit and vegetable crops, oilseeds, etc. To enterprises of the secondary processing of raw materials: bread, macaroni, confectionery, white sugar, secondary winemaking, tea making and cigarette making, oil processing enterprises (margarine, mayonnaise, soap) are included. The raw materials of these enterprises are products of primary processing enterprises: flour, powdered sugar, vegetable oil, wine materials, etc.

The more types of food industry products there are, the more diverse the raw materials are. Therefore, they can be divided into certain groups according to their main characteristics or chemical composition. For example, it is possible to divide into groups of dry plant raw materials and wet plant raw materials, or into groups of carbohydrate raw materials, oily raw materials, protein raw materials, and essential oil raw materials. Any raw material is a biomaterial, its specific properties are determined by indicators such as chemical composition, elements of cell and tissue structure. The chemical composition of these raw materials includes proteins, carbohydrates, lipids, vitamins, enzymes and microelements. The quality of raw materials belonging to each group is measured and determined by specific parameters. These quantities are divided into groups of quantities indicating physical, chemical, technological, organoleptic and other properties of raw materials. In particular, grain quality indicators are divided into five groups: botanical-physiological indicators - plant type, variety, germination period and amount, germination energy; organoleptic indicators - color, taste, smell; physical indicators - shape and size, absolute and natural weight, etc.; mechanical parameters - tensile modulus, dispersibility, viscosity, etc.; chemical indicators - moisture content, ash content, gluten content, acidity, etc.; technological indicators - special dimensions that indicate whether grain is suitable for flour production, bread production or pasta production.

Fruit raw materials are divided into 4 groups

according to their structure and production on the plant stem

divided into: seeds (apples, pears, citrus fruits), grains (cherries, cherries, plums, apricots), soft fruits (grapes, currants, raspberries) and nuts (almonds, walnuts , khandan pistachios). Raw materials are divided into 2 groups: vegetative - leaves, roots and stems (cabbage, lettuce, radish, onion, carrot, potato, beet, etc.) and fruits (pumpkin, cucumber, tomato, pea, etc.). Storage of raw materials is an organizational part of any technological process, its task is to store raw materials without loss or with minimal waste and to maintain or increase the quality of raw materials. The types of methods used in practice to solve the problem of storage of raw materials are as follows:

1. Preparation of raw materials for storage (cleaning from additives, dividing into pieces, combing or storage, etc.)

2. Drying of raw materials (grains and oilseeds) or canning (fruits and vegetables).

3. Creation and automatic management of optimal conditions in the environment

(composition, relative humidity, temperature).

4. Preventing the entry of various pests and insects (insects, rodents, birds).

5. Preparation of raw materials for production.

The implementation of these storage measures not only preserves the quantity of raw materials, but also preserves its technological quality and lays the foundation for the production of quality food products.

There are losses in the storage of raw materials until the processing period. These losses are of two types - loss in mass (reduced weight) and loss in quality (reduced content). Although these losses are interrelated, mass loss does not always affect quality (spill reduction). Storage losses of raw materials can be divided into five groups: mechanical, physical-chemical, biological, biochemical and chemical losses. Mechanical losses are mainly due to spillage, scattering, washing according to the physical properties of raw materials.

During the growth of plants, the processes of

synthesis of useful substances are mainly carried out in their leaves, stems, seeds and fruits, while in the storage of agricultural products mainly hydrolytic - decomposition processes take place. However, after harvesting, the raw materials undergo post-harvest ripening processes, in which the synthesis processes of the growing period come to an end. During the subsequent storage period, the raw material gradually undergoes the processes of the dormant stage from the post-harvest ripening stage. In such a natural state of rest, physiological processes are minimal and germination is not observed. However, in the process of respiration, oxidation-reduction reactions take place with the participation of enzymes, raw materials emit heat and carbon dioxide, toxins are broken down, and the immunity of raw materials increases. In this case, the consumption of raw materials is extremely low. The main factor in maintaining this condition is low temperature. The deterioration of the quality of raw materials, which has lost its peaceful state, accelerates. Depending on the type of these raw materials, they undergo biochemical and chemical processes of self-heating, physiological nausea and, at the last stage, germination, and become completely useless.

Raw material storage regimes are temperature, relative humidity and gas content of the environment. For example, there are three modes of storage of grain mass: in a dry state (up to critical moisture); in a cooled state; under oxygen-free conditions. In such regimes, it is possible to store grain for 3-4 months in enterprises, 2-3 years in silo elevators, and 4-5 years in special warehouses. Fruits and vegetables can be stored in a chilled state in two ways: chilled and frozen. The main condition for good storage of any fruit and vegetable is the optimally selected cooling temperature and relative humidity. For example, apples -0.5 to +0.50C; grains 00C; tangerine at temperatures from 0.3 to 20C and relative humidity of 80-85% for cereals; 85-90% for apples, grapes, pears; 78-83% is the optimal condition for citrus. Potatoes should not be cooled to 00C and below. There are no universal storage conditions for fruits and vegetables. The shelf life of any fruit and vegetable, even under optimal conditions, is its individual characteristic and has a certain limit. Fruits and vegetables such as apples, grapes, cabbage, and some varieties of onions can be stored for up to 6-7 months, while tomatoes, cucumbers, green vegetables, grains and soft fruits can be stored for several weeks or as long as 2-3 months. There are different methods of preparing raw materials for processing, and which method to use depends on the type of raw materials, their physical condition, and the method of further processing. In this case, the methods of preparation for processing of various dry and dispersed raw materials are similar, and the methods of preparation for processing of various aqueous raw materials are also similar.

ASSORTMENT OF MARGARINE PRODUCTS AND PRODUCTION TECHNOLOGY OF CULINARY OILS.

Margarine was produced as a butter-like fat in 1869 by the French chemist Maj-Muret. He proposed to emulsify the fast-dissolving part of melted beef fat using whey from the cow's stomach. When the mixture was cooled in cold water, a semi-solid light yellow shiny product was formed. Maj-Mure called it margarine. (Margaret is a French pearl). It means pearl. Margarine is an emulsion with small particles, which includes: fats, milk, salt, sugar, vitamins, phosphatides, emulsifiers, etc. The first margarine factories were launched in 1930 in Moscow and St. Petersburg. In our republic, hard and soft margarine is produced at the Tashkent oil-oil combine. The nutritional value of oils is determined by their energy value and physiological effect. Margarine is not inferior to milk fat in terms of absorption by the human body, and it is higher than it in terms of energy value.

It is known that oils in the state of fine-particle emulsion are good for the human body like It is also affected by the melting temperature of fats. Therefore, based on the characteristics of the oils used for margarine, the melting point of the product should not exceed 31-340C. Essential (unsaturated) fatty acids present in margarine increase its physiological value. Assortment of margarine products. Margarine products are divided into:

1. The amount of fat in margarines should not be less than 82%. (milk margarines).

2. Culinary oils contain up to 99.7% fat (for confectionery, bakery and cooking).

Depending on their use and recipe, margarines are divided into:

A) Kitchen and branded (sandwich) margarines

B) For industrial processing and general food system

C) margarines with flavoring additives (fat content should not be less than 62%).

Margarines can be hard, soft and liquid. Soft margarines are used as sandwich butter. Liquid margarine bread it is used for the production of flour confectionery products. Flavored margarines (chocolate) contain cocoa powder, a large amount of sugar, and are used for the preparation of confectionery products. Culinary oils are produced in the following assortment: for biscuits, chocolate and waffle products. These oils have different composition and consist of the following components: salomas, transesterified oil, vegetable oil. Beef fat is also added to some cooking oils. Oils used for bakery products are prepared in a liquid state with the addition of phosphatide. The main raw materials for the production of margarine. The main raw materials for margarine production are oil and milk. Fatty raw materials. The main raw material is a plant in a liquid and hydrogenated (healthy) state is oil. Sunflower, cotton and soybean oils are widely used. Hydrogenated oil is the main ingredient in the margarine product recipe. In addition, beef, sheep fat and butter are used as animal fats. Milk. Pasteurized or frozen milk is used for the production of margarine. Warmed milk gives margarine a unique taste and aroma, and increases the shelf life of margarine. The amount of solids in milk is more than 8.0 percent and the acidity is 210 It should be less than T (0.1H needed to neutralize 100ml of milk as Turner's acidity of milk if the acidity exceeds 230T, milk may coagulate during pasteurization. The acidity of freshly milked milk is 15-160T. About emulsions. Margarine is a thick emulsion made from a mixture of water and oil. Emulsion is a mixture of two liquids that do not mix and do not dissolve in each other. One of the liquids is distributed in the form of small particles (droplets) in the other. There are two types of emulsion: oil-in-water (O-W) and water-in-oil (W-O). Examples of natural emulsions are milk or butter. Emulsifiers are used to make the emulsion stable.

Emulsifier. In the preparation of margarine, an

emulsifier is used to create a stable and fine-particle emulsion. A good emulsifier makes margarine very stable, improves the binding of fats with water and the formation of complex compounds, emulsification properties, accelerates absorption into the body, and increases surface activity. Monoglyceride, monoglycerin distearate (T-2), dried milk and phosphatide concentrate mixture with monoglycerin (T-F), MG, MGD, T-1 brand emulsifiers are used as emulsifiers in the production of margarine.

Margarine recipe. The fat base of margarine consists of a mixture of different fats. The melting temperature, hardness and amount of solid phase of this mixture are the main indicators of margarine. The melting temperature depends on the composition of the fatty base. Several types of salomas with different melting temperatures, transesterified oils and liquid vegetable oils are added to the fatty base of margarine to create a moderate structure. Oil base recipes for confectionery, bread products and culinary oils are made depending on their use. The following tables show the recipe for milk margarine and soft margarine. Lactic acid is milk albumin, milk globulin. Casein can make up to

80% of the total amount of oxil. The presence of solids in milk represents the nutritional value of milk, and their decrease indicates that the milk has been diluted with water. Milk contains both fat-soluble and water-soluble vitamins and mineral elements. Milk is processed in two stages. The first is cleaning, the second is freezing. Milk is pasteurized to completely remove bacteria.

The purpose of freezing milk is to give margarine a milky, sour and aromatic taste and prevent the development of microflora that may be present in margarine under the influence of lactic acid. In a mixture of 1:1 and 1:3, thawed and non-thawed milk is added to margarine. The aroma of heated milk is determined by the presence of diacetyl and diacetoin substances. Milk freezing drops are brought to the margarine factory in dry form. First, a small amount of drops in a liquid form, then in a large amount of milk drops are prepared. All components are specially prepared according to this recipe. Phosphatide concentrate is used as an emulsifier and is added to increase the nutritional value of cooking oils. Phosphatide concentrate should contain not less than 50% phosphatide and moisture should not exceed 4%. It is dissolved in the following ratio oil:phosphatide=4:1. Table salt is added to improve the taste of margarine and as a preservative. Sugar improves the taste of margarine. Fatty solutions of carotene are added to margarine as dyes to give it a light yellow, i.e., butter-like color. Currently, carotene obtained by biosynthesis is used. Vitamins are added to increase the biological properties of margarine. Additional artificial flavorings are also added to give a pleasant aroma. The principle of margarine production. Margarine production consists of the following operations: grading, mixing, emulsifying, supercooling, crystallization and packaging. There are two methods of grading: by weight and volume. Standardization by weight ensures the correct amount of components. Mixing. In the process of mixing the components, mixers are used, which keep the temperature of the mixture at 38-40 0C. During mixing, coarse emulsion, i.e. preliminary emulsifistprts process is performed. The rotation speed of the mixer is 60 rev/min. Emulsification. Homogenizers are used to create a fine-particle emulsion from a coarse emulsion. They are horizontal triple plunger high pressure pumps. Their main element is the homogenizing chamber part. After the emulsion enters the chamber, it is squeezed out by means of a ratchet and a valve. At this time, a highly dispersed emulsion is formed. The high pressure created by the pump is used to overcome the resistance of the emulsion in the pipes from the supercooler to the packaging machine. The pressure of the pump is 18-22 atm. Super cooling. When the margarine emulsion is cooled, the crystallization process takes place. The formation of structures depends on the speed of cooling, the speed of mixing, and the amount of saturated and unsaturated glycerides. Large crystals are formed upon slow cooling. They give margarine the properties of roughness, brittleness and crumbliness. In modern margarine production enterprises, supercooling is carried out together with mixing. As a result, margarines that are quickly liquid, flexible and of good consistency are produced. Crystallizers are installed before packaging in order to obtain the required crystal structure and a product with a uniform and smooth consistency.

1. Dissolving fatty compounds included in the margarine recipe;

2. Preparation of salt-water solution and mixing

of emulsifier;

3. Mix the components until homogeneous and emulsify them;

4. Reserve the prepared emulsion;

4. Pasteurization of the finished emulsion at high temperature (in the production of margarine with a milk component)

5. Preparation of margarine from ready-made emulsion by supercooling method;

6. Sending the finished product for packing in boxes by pouring or in an automatic system.

The oil added according to the margarine recipe enters the tank (14), then with the help of a centrifugal pump (2) the meter (3) with a scale (13) is transferred, and the solid added according to the margarine recipe oil heater (1) melt in pump (2) comes down to the meter (3). On the other hand, salt water prepared in tank (10) is supplied here with the help of pump (2) and emulsifiers prepared by melting in tank (11) are supplied by pump (2). The resulting oil-salt water mixture is transferred to the coarse emulsion forming tank (4) by the pump (2), then the coarse emulsion is pumped through the pump (2) in the disperser (5) to form a homogeneous emulsion. is transmitted. The resulting homogeneous emulsion is transferred to tank (6) and through a plunger pump (7), it is pasteurized in a high-temperature pasteurizer (8) to remove microorganisms and enzymes from its contents. The pasteurized semi-finished product is cooled in a supercooler (vatator) (9). The finished product is sent to the packing shop for filling margarine in the form of briquettes in the static container (12), or the finished product sent directly to boxes for packing. If the prepared product does not meet the requirements, it is returned to the tank (6) intended for the finished emulsion for processing. In the production of margarine in a monolith, it is passed through a decrystallizer and put into boxes is filled. Most continuous automated lines have a capacity of 2.5 tons per hour. Bulk margarines contain a large amount of liquid vegetable oil. Casting margarines are produced with 82% and 60% fat. These margarines are intended for disease prevention and treatment. They are produced in polymer containers (glasses and ja

PROCESSING TECHNOLOGY OF

MAYONNAISE AND SALAD OIL.

Production of mayonnaise: Mayonnaise is an M-S type emulsion and is a food product and includes vegetable oil, dry milk, egg powder, sugar, salt and other nutritional and flavoring additives. It is used as an additional product to increase the satiety of food, increase appetite and improve digestion. Mayonnaise is a product of high biological value. It includes: 1) vegetable oils (sunflower, cotton, soybean oil). These oils are not only a source of calories, but also a source of essential acids (olein, linole). These acids help reduce the amount of cholesterol in the blood; 2) egg powder is a source of proteins, which is necessary to improve liver function. Basic raw materials for making mayonnaise: The main component of mayonnaise is refined deodorized vegetable oil. Salomas cannot be used because it breaks the emulsion. Dry milk or egg powder is used as an emulsifier. Dry milk is a structure-builder, which helps proteins dissolve in water and retain moisture. Mustard powder is a flavoring additive. The proteins in its composition provide emulsification. Salt and sugar are used as flavoring additives. Baking soda maintains a clear pH, which improves the curdling of milk proteins. Acetic acid is a flavoring additive that increases the bactericidal properties of mayonnaise. Water is used to dissolve salt and sugar, to dissolve and thicken proteins. The quality of liquid vegetable oils, sugar, milk, and salts are subject to the same requirements as in the production of margarine. Egg powder should not have a foreign smell and taste. Mustard powder should be dry and have a sharp allyl oil smell. Mayonnaise recipe and assortment: Mayonnaises are divided into kitchen, dietary and children's groups with added spices, flavoring and flavoring additives: - Kitchen ("Provençal", "Sudli", "Lyubitelsky") mayonnaises are more elegant and sour. to me, has a good viscosity and consistency.- Mayonnaises with added spices ("Bahor" with dill; "Gorchitsali", etc.) are similar in taste and flavor to "Provençal" mayonnaise, but added the taste and smell of the medicine is noticeable. These mayonnaises are used to add flavor to salads and vegetable, fish, and meat dishes. Mayonnaises with spicy, tasty and astringent additives are divided into groups with bitter and sweet taste.

The bitter ones include "Gorchichnyy", "Prazdnichnyy", "Ogonyok" and others, and the sweet ones include "Orange", "Honey" and others. These mayonnaises will have a sweet taste characteristic of the added essence. They use phosphate starch as a leavening agent, and these mayonnaises are used to flavor fruit and other salads. They are also used in children's food and as a sandwich product. "Diabetic" mayonnaise uses xylitol instead of sugar. This mayonnaise will have a sweet taste. The recipe of some mayonnaise is shown in the table. Mayonnaise production technology. Periodic and semi-continuous technological schemes are used in the production of mayonnaise.

The periodic method consists of the following steps: preparation of components, preparation of paste, preparation of "coarse" emulsion, preparation of finely dispersed emulsion, addition of aromatic and flavoring additives. Preparation of components. Spreadable components: dry milk, sugar, egg and mustard powders and salt, sieved in a vibrocell with a cell size of 1-3 mm. Vinegar acid saline solution is prepared in a special container. A clear saline solution with a first concentration of 13-15% is given there, then 80%

acetic acid is added in the required amount. The concentration of the solution should be 7-9%. Preparation of mayonnaise paste. Water of 90-1000C is poured into one of the mixers and mustard powder is added. Mustard powder: water ratio should be 1: (2-2.5). Mix until a homogeneous substance is formed. Then 35-400. Add water, dry milk, soda and sugar. Dry milk: water ratio should be equal to 1:3. Then steam is applied to the casing using a stirrer. For good melting of the components, the temperature is brought to 90-950C and held for 20-25 minutes. Then the mixture is cooled to 40-450C.

Egg powder and 40-450C water are added to the second mixer. Their ratio should be equal to 1:2. It is mixed and heated to 60-650C and held for 20-25 minutes. Then it is cooled to 30-400C. Getting mayonnaise on a small power line. Currently, the number of small companies producing mayonnaise is increasing. In order for the quality of the finished product to be at the required level and meet the standard requirements, it is necessary to use high-quality raw materials, equipment that ensures the formation of a durable emulsion, and to observe the technological regime and sanitary-hygienic requirements."Bagri" activator was developed and put into production for homogenization of coarse mayonnaise emulsion. The equipment consists of a conical rotor and a stator with a rotation frequency of 50 s-1.

The constructive structure of the equipment allows the production of high-quality, stable emulsion mayonnaise with moderate colloidal structure. Based on the "Bagri" activator, "Malish" lines with different production capacity have been created. Small businesses can be equipped with them.

Dry components are weighed on a scale (1) and mixed with the required amount of water according to the recipe in a mixer (2). Mayonnaise paste (3) is fed to the mixer (4) with the help of a pump and vegetable oil and vinegar solution are added according to the recipe. The mayonnaise emulsion is sent to the activator "Bagri" (8) through the block of filters (5) with the help of a pump. The resulting finely dispersed mayonnaise emulsion is fed to the container (7) intended for ready-made mayonnaise and transferred to the packaging machine. To increase the shelf life of the mayonnaise obtained on the

"Malish" line, production is achieved in aseptic conditions, that is, by pasteurization with a pot and aseptic packaging. For this, a mixer consisting of a special bath for long-term (60 minutes) pasteurization is carried out in "Bakelin". These devices consist of 4 electric heaters of the 0.86-0.1 type with a power of 3.15 kW, which are used for heating and pasteurization at 950C. In aseptic packaging, the used fixing materials are processed before use. The organoleptic properties of food products produced by aseptic technology increase and meet the physiological requirements of nutrition. Mainly used foreign aseptic packaging equipment.

CONCEPT OF MILK PROCESSING PRODUCTS. DAIRY PRODUCTS PRODUCTION TECHNOLOGY

Milk contains an average of 3.8% milk fat; 4.7% milk sugar; 3.3% oxyl; 0.7% minerals and 87.5% water. Doctors and scientists scientifically proved that milk and milk products are very important for the health of children, their mental and physical development. Therefore, providing the young generation with such products can be considered as an important means for them to grow up strong and mentally healthy and participate in the development of our country. This affects the milk sections. Mining cow's udder brings substances necessary for the production of milk from the arterial vessel. The milk ducts in the udder absorb these substances contained in the blood and as a result of the synthesis of the substances milk appears in the udders. So, how much milk is produced depends not only on the cow's feed and nutritional value, but also on the synthesis of substances in the udder. The production of milk and, in particular, the synthesis of its constituents is a very complex process. In this case, the special cells of the mammary gland absorb a certain amount of substances from the deposit, change them and synthesize the components of milk.

The udder produces milk continuously. Discharge of milk when the mammary gland becomes engorged stops and the produced components start to return. They are milked in time in order to preserve the milkiness of the cows. Cows give an average of 2500 kg of milk during the lactation period together with milk,

100 kg of fat, 85 kg of milk, 125 kg of milk sugar, 17 kg of mineral salts, all together, it separates about 320 kg of dry matter. Often, the amount of dry matter excreted by animals with high milk production is higher compared to its weight. Cow tukkach lactation period begins. Therefore, it is important to know when it starts. Pregnancy of cows lasts 9 months (280-285 days). If the time of natural and artificial calving is known, it is possible to calculate when the cow will give birth. Cow milking Cows are milked two or three times a day. Before milking, it is necessary to observe the sanitary requirements of the cow:

- wash the ash thoroughly with soap;

- wear a clean white robe;

- washing cow's udders with hot water (400C) and wiping with a hair brush;

- massage the udders for 35-40 seconds.

Reception and preliminary processing of milk High-quality raw milk can be used to produce high-quality milk products. High-quality raw milk refers to a complex of chemical composition, physico-chemical and microbiological indicators that determine the ability of milk to be processed. Milk from Kabul is processed. Milk processing includes the following processes: reception, cleaning, heat treatment, cooling, packaging and storage for a certain period.

When accepting milk, its chemical parameters and quantity that meet the standard requirements are taken into account. Milk is filtered to remove impurities. Various filters are used for cleaning: cotton filter, disks, gauze, synthetic materials, metal sieve and others. Purified milk is quickly cooled to stop the growth of microorganisms. In small enterprises, water is used to cool milk. Later, plate coolers are used to cool the milk. Milk with an acidity of 19-200T can be stored for a certain period (6 hours). In this case, the milk is heat treated. Heat treatment of milk is carried out at a temperature of 760C for 15-20 seconds. Milk after heat treatment it is quickly cooled to a temperature of 4-60C in a plate cooling unit.

Cooled milk whose temperature does not exceed 100C is sent to large milk production enterprises in airships or tankers. Standard requirements are observed when accepting milk. Cow milk is accepted according to the standard "Cow's milk, requirements at the time of purchase". According to the requirements of this standard, cow's milk was milked from a healthy cow, cooled to 20C and filtered within 2 hours after milking. should be At the time of receiving milk, the temperature of milk should not exceed 100C. In terms of appearance and consistency, milk should be a homogeneous liquid, yellowish-white in color, without lumps, density equal to 1027 kg/m3.

Depending on the physico-chemical and microbiological parameters, milk is divided into three types: high, first and second types.

These indicators of milk are presented in the following table. Conditions and methods of milk purification Received milk is purified to remove natural impurities (microorganisms) and mechanical impurities. Such cleaning is carried out in moving separators - milk cleaning equipment using gravity or pressure and centrifugal forces. During filtering, milk must withstand the resistance of metal and fabric filter cloths. After the liquid has passed through the filter tubes, these tubes retain the impurities in the milk. That's why every 15-20 minutes the waste in the filter is separated. Milk cleaners working under pressure are used to clean milk from mechanical impurities.

The effectiveness of milk purification depends on this pressure. Milk enters the cleaning unit at a pressure of 2×105 Pa.

Milk contains milk plasma and foreign waste particles. Due to the difference between the density of these particles, milk is purified in these devices. The density of extraneous waste is high compared to milk plasma, so they are centrifugal under the influence of force, it comes to the wall of the drum. Separator - in the milk cleaning unit, the milk is taken to the cleaning stage.

The milk supplied for cleaning falls into the plate holder with a central tube of the device. Sungra milk is drawn from the bushing between the saucer holder and the saucers

the drum is pushed up and comes out through the hole in the drum cover. The process of cleaning milk starts in the plate holder and ends in the gaps between the plates. In order to reduce the mechanical waste in milk in these devices, milk is 30-

Cleaned at a temperature of 450C Currently, plate heaters are used for continuous heating of milk.

Cooling the milk.

The temperature of milk arriving at the enterprise is up to 100 C. Freshly milked milk contains certain bactericidal substances, which not only stop the activity of bacteria in milk, but also destroy them. But such bactericidal substances are resistant to high temperatures. If the milk is not cooled quickly, they curdle easily. As a result, microorganisms that cause fermentation in uncooled milk quickly multiply. Therefore, it is advisable to cool the milk brought to the enterprise. At a temperature of 320 C, the acidity of milk increases 2.8 times in 10 hours, and the number of bacteria in it increases as much. Acidity and number of bacteria do not change in milk cooled to 1200 C for 10 hours.

In order to prevent deterioration of milk quality during storage, it is quickly cooled to a temperature of 4-50C.

A plate cooler is used to cool milk. Water, salt solution and cold water are used as coolants.

1.2. Milk separation

It varies depending on the amount of fat in the milk taken. Milk can be full fat, medium fat or fat free. In order to normalize the amount of fat in milk, it is mechanically processed. That is, from the separator to extract the fat contained in milk is transferred and this oil is homogenized to break the globules into smaller particles.

Separation means separating milk into two fractions with different densities: high-fat (cream) and low-fat (skimmed milk). Separation of milk is carried out in a separator - cream separator unit. Milk is separated at a temperature of 45-50C. Fats are separated from milk plasma under the influence of centrifugal force generated as a result of the rotation of the separator drum. Using a special mechanism separated cream and skimmed milk are removed from the separator.

The scheme of dividing milk into cream and skimmed milk in the separator is shown in the picture below.

In this case, the milk is absorbed from the central part of the drum and spreads in a thin layer in the gaps between the plates. Under the influence of centrifugal force, fat balls in milk accumulate on the surface of the plates and float up towards the moving edge of the drum. Under the influence of this force, the heavier part of the milk is pushed to the outer part of the drum. The separated cream moves towards the special outlet hole with the inner part of the separating plates of the drum and is taken out through the hole. And skim milk is a separator it passes through the gap between the inner surface of the plates and exits through the hole installed in them. Skimmed milk contains 0.05% fat. The degree of defatting of milk depends on a number of factors. These are:

1. Cleanliness and freshness of milk. How little mechanical waste is in the milk and the lower the acidity, the better the separator works. The presence of such waste in milk reduces the degree of defatting of milk.

2. Size of oil balls. The more fat globules in milk, the more cream is extracted from it. The size of fat balls in milk should be very small. If the size of fat globules is close to 1 nm, cream cannot be separated from such milk.

3. Milk temperature. The optimal temperature

for separation is considered to be 45-50C. A decrease in temperature worsens the separation of fat globules in milk. Because the viscosity of separated milk is expected quickly. As a result, the resistance in the gap between the plates increases. This slows down the movement of fat globules and reduces the level of defatting of milk.

4. The frequency of rotations of the drum - a change in the frequency of rotations of the separator drum, that is, a decrease, leads to a decrease in the indicator of the milk separation effect. The frequency rotation of the drum should be uniform. 5. The amount of fat in milk - the more fat in the milk, the more cream is separated as a result of separation.

Milk packaging

Cleaned, normalized and homogenized and pasteurized milk is sent to the last process of packaging. Pasteurized milk is produced in glass bottles, paper bags, polyethylene bags in 0.25, 0.5, 1 liters. Packaging of pasteurized milk in small bottles is carried out on automatic lines.

Currently, packing of milk in polyethylene and paper bags is widely used. Such bags are very convenient to use, they do not require a complicated washing process, and their transportation is considered very light.

Packaging of milk in paper bags is carried out on AP1-N and AP2-N automatic devices. The capacity of such automatic equipment is to pack 3000-9000 bags per hour. The temperature of the packaged milk was 80C and the relative humidity of the air was 85-90%.

can be stored in refrigerators for up to 18 hours. The prepared product is subjected to technological and microbiological control. According to the requirements of the standard, the taste and smell of pasteurized milk should be higher than 210 T of freshly milked milk, and the level of purity should not be lower than the first group.

Milk processing and storage technology

Milk processing and storage technology involves a series of steps to ensure the quality, safety, and shelf life of milk and dairy products from farm to consumer. This comprehensive process includes various stages such as collection, pasteurization, homogenization, and storage. Here's an overview of milk processing and storage technology:1. Milk Collection and ReceptionCollection: Milk is collected from dairy farms either directly by dairy processors or through cooperative collection centers.Reception: Upon arrival at the processing plant, milk undergoes initial testing for quality parameters such as temperature, acidity (pH), and visual inspection for contaminants.2. Filtration and StandardizationFiltration: Milk may be filtered to remove any particulate matter or impurities that could affect product quality.Standardization: The fat content of milk is adjusted by separating cream (to make higher fat products like cream and butter) or by adding cream to produce products like whole milk.3. PasteurizationPurpose: Heat treatment to destroy harmful pathogens (bacteria, viruses) and enzymes while preserving milk's nutritional quality.Methods:High-Temperature Short-Time (HTST): Heating milk to 72°C (161.6°F) for 15 seconds.Ultra-High Temperature (UHT): Heating milk to 135-150°C (275-302°F) for a few seconds, extending shelf life without refrigeration.

4. HomogenizationPurpose: Breaks down fat globules in milk to prevent cream separation, creating a uniform consistency and texture.process: Milk is forced through small openings under high pressure, evenly distributing fat particles throughout the milk.5. Cooling and StorageCooling: Pasteurized milk is rapidly cooled to refrigeration temperatures (around 4°C or 39°F) to inhibit bacterial growth and maintain freshness.storage: Stored in stainless steel tanks under controlled temperature and hygiene conditions to preserve quality before further processing or packaging.6. PackagingPackaging Types: Milk is packaged in various formats including cartons, bottles, pouches, and bulk containers.aseptic Packaging: Ensures milk remains sterile during packaging, extending shelf life and maintaining nutritional integrity.7. Quality Control and TestingTesting: Regular checks for bacteria count, antibiotics, acidity levels, and sensory evaluation ensure product safety and quality.traceability: Tracking systems ensure milk batches can be traced back to farms, enhancing food safety and accountability.8. Transportation and DistributionTemperature

Control: Maintaining cold chain logistics to prevent spoilage and maintain freshness during transportation to retailers or consumers.Distribution: Efficient logistics to ensure timely delivery and minimize product handling.9. Emerging TechnologiesMicrofiltration and Membrane Technology: Used for milk clarification and concentration, preserving vitamins

1.6. Bacterial drugs and drop preparation technology

There are a number of dairy products in which a certain type of microorganisms is used in the production technology. These are: milk - yeast products, cheese, sour cream, etc.

At the time of development, microorganisms destroy its enzymes, actively affect the milk plasma and cause biochemical changes. Milk products subjected to such microbiological effects are called fermented. Specially selected and grown pure cultures are used in the production of fermented products. A number of types and strains of microorganisms that are useful for technological conditions are included in pure cultures. Isolated strains are stored in special collections. When necessary, they are taken from collections and used to prepare bacterial zakvaska or concentrates. Microorganisms selected and prepared under special aseptic conditions are placed in a nutrient medium. The grown bacteria are concentrated in special centrifuges together with the nutrient broth. After the quality of the prepared biomass is thoroughly checked, it is packaged in aseptic conditions and sent to milk production enterprises in frozen or liquid form. They are shipped dry to distant places.

Milk production technology

Milk is produced in a wide range. They differ from each other in chemical composition and heat treatment. They are as follows:

1. Pasteurized milk

2. Sterilized milk

3. Boiled milk. Natural milk with a fat content of 4.5-6%

4. Standardized milk, i.e. defatting milk with the amount of fat in it or

3.2% milk delivered by creaming

5. Reconstituted milk. This milk is made from dry milk. Dry milk is dissolved in water and stored for a certain period of time for the oxils to bend. Sungra is coarsely filtered.

6. Fat milk - increase the fat content to 6% with the addition of cream

is prepared.

7. Skimmed milk is milk from which fat has been removed by passing natural milk without cream.

8. Acidified milk. It is prepared by mixing dry or condensed milk with skimmed milk. Its protein content is significantly higher than that of ordinary natural milk.

9. Vitaminized milk. Vitamins are added to non-cream milk.

10. Cocoa or coffee milk. Milk made with 2.5% cocoa or 2% coffee.

For the production of milk, the following technological processes are carried out: receiving milk, cleaning, cooling, standardization, homogenization, pasteurization and packaging.

Pasteurized milk production technology

The following types of pasteurized milk are produced:

1) Pure normalized (2.5-3.2% fat content) milk.

2) Vitaminized (contains 2.5-3.2% fat content and ascorbic acid) milk.

3) Oily (6% fat content) milk.

The milk used for the production of pasteurized milk is from mechanical waste

is cleaned. Sungra milk is preheated to a temperature of 40-45 0C. Skimmed milk or cream is added to milk heated to a temperature of 40-45 0C, and the amount of fat in it is adjusted.

Milk is homogenized in order not to separate the fat content and to obtain a homogeneous product. Homogenization is carried out at a temperature of 62-63 0C and a pressure of 12.5-15 MPa. Homogenized milk is pasteurized at a temperature of 76-78 0C for 15-20 seconds. Sungra is cooled to a temperature of 4-6 0C. Pasteurized and cooled milk is put into glass bottles or polythene bags and cans, and then it is packaged, labeled and stored.

GENERAL FOR THE PRODUCTION OF MIXED FEED

INFORMATION

Uzbekistan is one of the ancient centers of animal husbandry. Soil and natural-climatic conditions of the republic - fertile irrigated lands, endless hills, steppe-desert and foothill pastures are favorable for the development of cattle breeding. Cattle breeding, pig breeding, poultry breeding, rabbit breeding, sheep breeding, goat breeding, goat breeding, camel breeding, poultry breeding, and fishing in water reservoirs are mainly developed in the irrigated lands.

An important factor in the development of animal husbandry is the creation of a solid feed base. Annual and perennial grasses, turnips (beets), turnips (pumpkin, watermelon), cereals (oats, barley, corn) are planted in the irrigated areas of the republic in order to provide stable feed for livestock. The area of fodder crops is 7.7% of the total agricultural land in the republic. With the expansion of grain fields in the republic, the amount of hay for livestock has increased dramatically.

At the beginning of 1995, there were 5.5 million cattle, 10 million cattle in all categories of farms in Uzbekistan. sheep and goats, 350 thousand pigs, 144.8 thousand horses, 84 thousand rabbits, 11 mln. there was poultry. Cattle breeding is in the main place in the republic's animal husbandry (74% of the total meat produced, 99.9% of milk). In the climatic conditions of Uzbekistan, milk, milk-meat and meat cattle breeds are raised. Cattle breeding for meat is developed in mountain and sub-mountain regions.

In the republic, sheep breeding for leather, meat, fat and wool has developed. Humpbacked Hisori sheep are raised mainly in mountain and sub-mountain regions (Surkhandarya, Kashkadarya and Jizzakh regions). Goats are raised for meat, curd and curative milk, wool, leather and tweed. Goats are raised in the highlands and sub-mountain regions. Goat breeding is developed in Namangan, Surkhandarya, Kashkadarya and Samarkand regions. Until the 1930s, the population of Uzbekistan was supplied with meat by small and scattered slaughterhouses and poultry houses. Currently, the republic's meat industry has its own independent and sufficient base of raw materials. In the next 10 years, the growth of the meat industry is ensured by maintaining and increasing the number of livestock in the republic. Republic dairy enterprises produce butter, milk-yogurt, canned milk, dry milk, cheese, brinza, cream, casein and other products. The production of milk products for small children and artificial milk (substitute for mother's milk) for feeding calves has been launched at dairy enterprises. The republic has developed on the basis of the poultry industry, chickens (eggs, meat), turkeys for meat, partially ducks, geese, and quails for dietary food are raised in the farms. 62 species of fish live in the rivers and tributaries of the republic. Chinoz Omixta Feed Production Enterprise produces fish meal from fish. The population's demand for food products and the industry's demand for raw materials are increasing day by day. In order to fully satisfy this, it is necessary to continuously raise the agricultural production, in particular, livestock breeding, which is its main sector. The production of mixed fodder in our country is increasing year by year. Its range is expanding and its biological effectiveness is increasing. Rapid development of mixed fodder industry, turning into a developed industry, shows that the use of mixed fodder is of great economic importance. Animals need all substances for normal life. About 50 chemical elements were found in their body, including: nitrogen, carbon, iodine, potassium, oxygen, calcium and others. 95 percent of them by mass are carbon, oxygen, hydrogen and nitrogen. A similar composition is found in plants.

These four elements are present in animal and plant bodies in different proportions and form many substances. The main task of mixed fodder plants is to supply feed containing the necessary amount of substances for the normal growth and development of the animal organism. General information on the production of mixed fodder. Plant and animal products, as well as mineral substances, are feed for farm animals. In animal husbandry, feed is divided into coarse, liquid, concentrated, mineral and various production wastes, depending on their origin, consistency and nutritional value.

In order to increase its efficiency in the use of fodder, it is possible to achieve it when feeding animals with them in the form of mixed fodder, and not by feeding them separately. Mixed feed is a product obtained by processing 6-12 types of different feed products (components, ingredients) according to the recipe. The ingredients used for the production of mixed feed are cleaned, dehulled and, if necessary, ground, then they are measured and mixed. Mixed feed is produced depending on the type, age and feeding purpose of farm animals, poultry and fish. Mixed fodder contains all the necessary nutrients for domestic animals. If mixed fodder is included in the diet, the productivity of animals, poultry and ruminants will increase significantly, they will grow and develop better, and their life activity will increase. If the daily ration of animals and poultry is always the same, then their productivity will decrease, the growth and development of young animals will be delayed, the life activity will slow down, and the incidence of various diseases will increase. feed in the form of briquettes, granules and galettes.Spreadable feed is a fairly uniform ground product. In the production of spreadable feed, the ingredients are cleaned of foreign impurities, dehulled, and ground. The ingredients prepared in this way are passed through a rater and a mixer. Briquettes are octagonal in shape, length 160-170 mm, width 70-80 mm, thickness 30-60 mm. For their production, a mixture of ground hay with ground ingredients is prepared. The obtained liquid mass falls into a special mixer, and at the same time, standardized and dispersed molasses are transferred from it. A mass consisting of a mixture of ground ingredients, hay and molasses is fed into presses and briquetted. Granular (granular) feed exhibits a fluid mass called granules, consisting of small cylinders of a certain diameter and height. In the production of granules, two methods are used: dry and wet. Granular mixed feed is usually used to feed poultry and pond fish. Galettes are rectangular in shape with holes. For the production of galettes, a dispersible mixed fodder is first taken, then leavened dough is made from it galets are baked and dried. Mixed fodder is divided into two main groups according to its composition and feed value: complete rations and concentrates. Chemical composition of mixed feed. Almost all substances necessary for a normal life animals get through food products. Animals in the organism 50 chemical elements were found: nitrogen, carbon, hydrogen, oxygen, calcium, phosphorus, sodium, potassium, sulfur, iron, iodine, cobalt, copper, manganese, etc. 95% of them by weight are carbon, oxygen, hydrogen and nitrogen. Plants have a similar composition. These four in the animal organism and plants an element exists in different proportions and forms many substances. This substances are grouped into groups, which are presented in the scheme below. Importance of different nutrients in feed. Dry matter. When organizing standardized feeding for animals, it is necessary to take into account their need for dry matter and the amount of dry matter in the ration. The amount of dry matter in food or ration is an important indicator of satiety. Animals get their daily calories and energy from the dry substances in the mixed feed included in the diet. These dry substances are an important source for the animal's body, and it is considered as food that increases the growth, development and productivity of the body. The efficiency of dry matter consumption depends on many factors; It depends on the variety of nutrients in the diet, the structure of the diet (type of feeding), energy concentration, the quality of food, their taste and physical properties, their preparation for eating, the level of productivity of animals, how nutrients are digested, etc. How difficult is the digestion of dry matter in the diet animals, especially high-yielding cattle, consume less of it. For example, in the diet when feeding dairy cows The amount of digestible dry matter should be at least 60 percent need Consumption of dry matter in the diet by animals addition, the composition of the diet and its necessary nutrients It also depends on whether it is balanced with substances. It's totally worth it is the basis of nutrition. High-yielding cows require more energy concentration per 1 kg of dry matter of the ration. Exchangeable energy and feed units.

Carbohydrates, fats and proteins are considered as a source of energy metabolism. The amount of energy metabolism depends on the ratio and concentration of the main nutrients in the diet, their digestibility and absorption.

Protein. Protein is very important in animal nutrition is of great importance. The main component of every living organism part is made up of proteins. The living activity of animals is related to the creation and decomposition of protein substances in their organism. A moderate amount of these oxygen substances in the animal's body improves digestion. It creates more activity in the body. Cows need to get enough protein in their diet to make their own body protein and milk protein. The quality of dietary protein, called proteins, varies. Wet protein contains proteins and amides, i.e. nitrogen compounds that are not characteristic of proteins. Amino acids in food are found not only in protein, but also in free form. According to zootechnical analysis, free amino acids belong to the conditional groups of amides. Some amino acids are considered non-exchangeable, that is, amino acids cannot be replaced by others in feed, and their deficiency leads to a decrease in animal productivity and a violation of metabolism. Therefore, the biochemical constituents of the mixed feed are always controlled in the production technology of the mixed feed. Non-exchangeable amino acids include lysine, tryptophan, histidine, leucine, isoleucine, phenylalanine, threonine, includes methionine, valine, arganine. These acids are in the animal body cannot be formed from other nitrogenous substances. They are taken into the animal body only with food. Proteins that have little or no amino acids are called incomplete proteins. Some amino acids, such as glycine, serine, cystine, proline, tyrosine, can be produced in the animal body from nitrogenous compounds taken in with food. Non-exchangeable amino acids in ruminants produced by microorganisms in the foregut. That is why such animals are less sensitive to protein quality compared to ruminant animals and poultry. The importance of methionine, tryptophan and lysine in the nutrition of productive cattle is extremely high. When feeding pigs, it is necessary to normalize the amount of lysine and methionine with cystine. In addition to free amino acids, the group of amides includes nitrogen-retaining glucosides, amides of amino acids, organic bases, nitrates and ammonia salts. The satiety of amides varies. Amino acids are close to proteins in terms of their content, but their amides are less saturated. 25-30 percent or more of the total amount of protein in green, silage, and root crops is contributed by amides, and in mixed feeds, the protein consists mainly of proteins.

The role of the rumen and its bacteria and

infusoria in the assimilation of dietary nitrogenous substances in ruminants is big. These microorganisms use nitrogenous substances, carbohydrates and minerals in animal feed for nutrition.

It should also be noted that bacteria use ammonia from nitrogenous substances to make their body's protein. The dying bacteria enter the chyme in the stomach and intestines and are digested together with the undigested food protein. absorbed into the blood through the wall.

Mineral substances. Although minerals have no energy value, they are of great importance in animal nutrition. Because they take an active part in all the processes of metabolism in the body. In order to properly feed animals, it is necessary to regulate the amount of calcium, phosphorus, sodium, chlorine, magnesium, potassium, sulfur, iron, zinc, manganese, copper, cobalt, iodine in the diet. In some cases, it is necessary to take into account the amount of fluorine, bromine, selenium, and molybdenum in the diet. In addition, in recent years, due to environmental pollution and the use of chemical and microbiological technology in the production of additional feed it is important to take into account the amount of mercury, lead, strontium in the diet.

It is also necessary to take into account the complex relationship of mineral substances with each other and with other feeding factors in the organization of complete feeding of animals. It has been found that there is a very close relationship between calcium, phosphorus and magnesium, between zinc and copper, potassium and magnesium, sodium and potassium, copper and iron, sulfur, copper and molybdenum. The need of animals for mineral substances depends on many factors, first of all, the relationship of certain elements to each other during the exchange process, their absorption and excretion level, and the amount of accumulation in the body.

Vitamins. Vitamins to ensure the proper functioning of the body, healthy growth of animals, their high productivity and the normalization of reproductive functions

It is considered very necessary. The role of vitamins is particularly important in the rapid development of animal husbandry. If there is a lack of any vitamin in the diet, the cattle's productivity will decrease and there will be a violation of metabolism in their body.

Evaluation of the nutritional value of mixed fodder Evaluation of the nutritional value of mixed fodder and digestibility of mixed fodder is determined on the basis of special experiments performed on animals. The digestibility of individual nutrients of mixed feed is expressed in percentages. The digestion process is different in different animals. Therefore, different types of animals digest the same mixed feed differently. The nutritional value of each mixed feed is characterized by the final result of feeding, i.e. productivity. The nutritional value of mixed feed and feed products is feed unit and it is equivalent to the nutritional value of 1 kg of oats with a moisture content of 13% and a volume weight of 450-480 g/m. Taking into account the importance of protein in animal feed, the wet protein content index is used in the evaluation of feed products along with the feed unit. When evaluating mixed feed, the number of feed units is taken in relation to 100 kg of mixed feed, and the amount of wet protein is expressed as a percentage. The nutritional value of feed for poultry is in kilocalories per 100 g of feed is evaluated by the amount of energy exchanged. Energy is divided into gross (total), exchangeable and productive types, depending on the amount in the mixture and the level of use by the organism. The total amount of heat produced by the combustion of food outside the body is called gross energy. A part of the exchangeable energy is used to support exchangeable processes in the body, and the rest - pure or productive energy - is spent on the production of products. Estimating mixed feed by the amount of exchangeable energy is a relatively simple and accurate method. This method shows how much of the feed's energy is spent on growth, egg production, body temperature control, and other physiological processes in the bird. The nutritional value of fur animals is estimated by the caloric value of 100 g of mixed feed, the amount of wet protein, fiber and micro-additives. Also, the amount of individual amino acids, fiber, minerals and vitamins is taken into account when assessing the nutritional value of mixed feed. In addition, there are technological indicators of the quality of mixed fodder: the size of crushing, the amount of whole seeds of spiked plants, the amount of metallomagnetic compounds. The quality of mixed fodder is regulated on the basis of state standards and technical conditions. Depending on the designation of mixed fodder (for large horned animals, calves, pigs for meat, chickens, laying hens, etc.), the nutritional value of it and various feed products varies widely. The maximum inclusion standards of individual components are established in the mixed feed of animals of different species and ages.

GRAIN QUALITY, MAIN INDICATORS AND METHODS OF THEIR DETERMINATION

The main quality indicators of grains include their freshness (color, taste, smell), moisture, size, degree of contamination, whether or not they are damaged by pests, vitreousness of the grain section, the amount of flower bark, etc. Grain is mainly brought to storage and processing in a certain volume. Grain masses are required to be uniform in appearance and quality. Determining grain quality is studied mainly in two groups. It is checked by organoleptic and laboratory methods. The laboratory method determines the moisture content of grains, the level of contamination with foreign substances, and the level of damage by warehouse pests. In order to get more detailed information about grain, parameters such as density of grain, mass of 1000 grains, vitreousness of grain kernel, protein content, amount and quality of gluten, and ash content in grain can also be determined. In the laboratory method, inspection works are mainly carried out with the help of special tools. Another way to determine grain quality is called the organoleptic method

includes evaluation using . In this method, it is possible to determine quality indicators that cannot be determined by other methods (for example, grain color, smell, taste). Determining grain purity indicators (color, smell, taste) are its main purity indicators. In addition to the main grain, the mass of grain presented in each batch may contain other impurities (weed seeds, sand, clay, stalks, husks, etc.). Therefore, it is necessary to pay attention to these when determining the quality of grain or determining the degree of purity. If defects or defects in the grain are detected, the defect category may be assigned and cases of return of the grain by the recipient may occur. Today, it is grown in our Republic,

A new UzDSt 880:2004 state standard for prepared and delivered wheat grain was developed and approved. This standard is used for wheat grains prepared in the state system and used for food and technical purposes. According to the requirements of this standard, the sample of wheat grain should be 750 g/l. The amount of water should not exceed 14%, the amount of foreign impurities should not exceed 1%, and the mixture of other grains should not exceed 3.0%, and other basic and important indicators are indicated. As indicated in the standards of the Russian Federation and the Republic of Kazakhstan, even in our standards for grains, it is not allowed to damage grains by warehouse pests, and measures against this are regularly considered. As we mentioned above, the selection and separation of samples is carried out in accordance with UzDSt to determine the color, taste and smell of grain.

Grain quality indicators:

The uniformity of grain sizes is one of the main indicators used to assess their quality. The more uniform the grains are in size, the higher the quality of cereal and flour products made from them, and the less waste from processing. To determine this indicator, grain is sifted in sieves of certain sizes. Grain color. In agriculture, the color of grains is their main quality indicator. Because depending on the color, it is possible to get a lot of information (for example: the type, variety, homogeneity of the grain) and other indicators are determined. The color of each grain is unique and reflects additional shine, lines and other indicators. The grain color should match the standards. Grain color is determined by comparison with standards or samples. Density (kg/m3) is one of the main indicators of grain, and this indicator depends on the structure, completeness, level of ripeness and other indicators of grain. Their density is due to the low amount of endosperm in whole grain will be relatively small. The density of fully ripe grains is slightly higher than the density of unripe grains.

The smell. Grain will have a unique smell. If the grain has a special smell, it is the grain it indicates that it is damaged and deteriorated. As for the reasons for the appearance of foreign odors in grain, it can be caused by absorption of various substances from the external environment, i.e., steam and gases, or other seeds mixed with grain, organic compounds, and various pests. 60 Determining the degree of vitreousness of grain. If the cross-sectional surface of the grains is completely vitreous or less than 1/4 of the vitreous cross-section surface, such grains are called vitreous grains. In floury grains, the cross-section is completely floury or less than 1/4 of the cross-section is vitreous. This indicator is determined in wheat, barley, corn and rice grains. According to the standard requirements, wheat grains are divided into small types based on the glassiness index.

Taste. Grains that are healthy in every way often have a unique taste

it has a sweet or slightly sweet taste. 100 g of grain is used to determine the taste index. Grain taste is defined in clean and ground grain. 100g of grain is brought, cleaned and ground in a mill, then chewed from 2g. It is necessary to rinse the mouth thoroughly before and after each determination. Determining the taste of grain is another organoleptic

It is conducted and studied in cases where it is not possible to determine the purity level of the grain according to the indicators.

We got acquainted with methods of storage of grain mass and checking of quality levels. When the grain mass is kept below the critical moisture content, metabolism, respiration and all other physiological processes in the grain are sharply reduced. When the grain mass is stored in this way, all its properties are fully preserved for a long time. If the grain mass is well cleaned and protected from external factors, it can be stored in warehouses for 4-5 years and in threshing floors for 2-1 years without any additional processing. When the pile of grain is kept dry, it is necessary to constantly monitor it.

Because with the creation of favorable conditions, the activity of microorganisms and pests can increase, and the grain can heat up by itself. The relative humidity of the air is also important. Grains and legumes are stored in warehouses with a moisture content of 12-14% can be stored for a long time. The amount of oil in the grain of oilseed crops is best determined when the moisture content is 6-11%. It is known that each grain or seed is important in agriculture. in addition to its characteristics, it has productivity, vegetation period, resistance to diseases and pests, and various consumption indicators. For example, different varieties of wheat have their own flour yield and baking quality indicators. Many varieties and hybrids of corn have clearly expressed technological properties and value. Flaxseed contains high-quality oil, and the amount of oil in sunflower seeds varies greatly depending on the variety.

Approximately 65-75% of food products consumed by humans are made from I grains. Many primary products such as flour, groats and fodder are produced from grain. The demand of our people for these products is extremely high. Satisfying the population's demand for grain and grain products is one of the most important tasks in the period of stabilization of the current market relations. It is not possible to fully satisfy the demand for grain and grain products only by growing a lot of grain. It is necessary to be able to store the grown grains, cereals and fine fodder without allowing wastage.

PRODUCTION TECHNOLOGY OF CANNED MILK

Milk is very important. But because milk contains a lot of water, it is considered a perishable product. Milk is processed to make it convenient to transport and store it over long distances. Processed milk products include canned milk. Canned milk is divided into condensed and dry milk depending on the production method.

The following processes are carried out for the production of milk preserves: reception of raw materials, cleaning, cooling and packaging, standardization, heat treatment, homogenization, condensing. Milk is the main raw material for the preparation of milk preserves. Milk delivered for canning is accepted according to quality indicators.

The received milk should not have different smell and taste, acidity should be 18-20°C, the size of the fat balls in it should be very small and uniform. The quality-rated and received milk is divided into paptias and the size is taken into account. Sungpa is sent to purify the milk. In this process, the milk content is cleaned from various wastes (in milk-cleaning devices), homogenized. Cleaned and homogenized milk is sent to storage and cooling. If milk 4-8 If cooled to 0C, it can be stored for 12 hours. In this case, milk is regulated and heat treated is sent to the vacuum apparatus. The essence of heat treatment is to destroy the microorganism contained in milk while keeping the biological value of milk. Heat treatment 1000C is carried out at a temperature. Microorganism-free milk at a temperature of 50-700C vacuum-it is condensed in the evaporating apparatus to reduce the amount of water in the milk. Annealing takes 18-20 hours.

Condensed milk cans

Condensed milk cans, sweetened condensed milk, condensed cream, and colored condensed milk assortments are produced. Condensed milk cans its chemical composition includes protein (up to 10%), milk fat (about 20%) and carbohydrates (44-85%). Condensed milk cans are very nutritious. 100 grams of sweetened condensed milk has 1440 kJ. Condensed milk with sugar. is produced. According to the chemical composition, the composition of such canned milk is 26.5% water, 43.5% sucrose, 28.5% dry matter and 8.5% milk fat. The production process of sweetened condensed milk follows the following sequence: reception of raw materials, purification; standardization, homogenization and pasteurization; preparation and addition of sugar syrup; condensing, cooling, packaging and storing the mixtur In the production of sweetened condensed milk, the most important of the above processes is sugar extraction. The added sugar affects the quality of the finished product. Dry sugar and milk put in the form of juice. Addition of solid sugar to milk leads to simplification of the technological process, reduction of equipment and energy consumption and fermentation time. but regardless of that, sugar is added in bulk to pasteurized milk

Microorganisms in sugar can fall and the quality of the finished product will deteriorate. In addition, when sugar is added in solid form, the viscosity of condensed milk increases rapidly during storage. Therefore, the purpose is to dissolve the sugar and drink it without juice is appropriate. Sifted sugar is dissolved in boiling water at a temperature of 70-800C, then heated until the juice boils. Inversion of sugar in juice at temperatures above 1000C possible To avoid this, the prepared juice is quickly added to the milk. Sugary juice is filtered in filters before adding to milk. Milk with added sugary juice is continued to ferment. Boiling is carried out until the amount of water in the mixture increases to 29-31%. Condensed milk from the vacuum apparatus is cooled. Two technological issues are solved when cooling condensed milk with sugar: product cooling and crystallization of milk sugar. Lactose in condensed milk begins to crystallize during cooling. Product after cooling, the crystallization process also stops. Normalized milk is homogenized before condensing in order to reduce the rate of formation of an oxidized fat layer during storage of the finished product. Homogenization It is carried out at a temperature of 65-75 0C under a pressure of 10-12 MPa (Fig. 16). The principle of sequential operation of equipment in the preparation of sweetened condensed milk according to the following: pure milk brought in tankers and accepted for its quality is sent to a special tank (5) for heat treatment through a pump. From here, a certain part of the milk goes to various milk cleaning equipment with a pump (1). In this case, milk is a waste product cleaned and directed to heat exchanger (7) for heat treatment. In this device, milk is homogenized at a temperature of 65-70C under a pressure of 10-12 MPa and various sent to a container (8) intended for purposes. The second part of pure milk flows through the pump into a container (9) intended for different purposes. Milk pump (1) orka it is sent to the heat exchanger (10), where it undergoes pasteurization and homogenization processes, and then in the cream separator (11), pure milk is separated into cream and skimmed milk. This a certain amount is separated from both products according to the recipe and homogenized in the heat exchanger (12). The homogenized product (8) is poured over the pure homogenized milk in the container. The products are thoroughly mixed and the amount of water contained is evaporated through the pump (1).It is sent to the vacuum apparatus (14) for condensing to 26-29%. The degree of condensation: 65-700S in the 1st case, 50-550S in the 2nd case. The annealing process is considered the last stage of product preparation. To find out how much the product is thickened, a small sample is taken from the vacuum apparatus and the amount of dry matter in it is analyzed in a refractometer. The condensation process at the end, the previously measured and prepared sugary juice is added and the condensation is continued again. condensation lasted 18-20 hours. Then the sweetened condensed milk is quickly cooled in a vacuum cooler (19) until the temperature reaches 18-20C. As a result of cooling, the product thickens by 2-3%, and its viscosity increases by 2-3 times. Lactose in sweetened condensed milk is partially crystallized. Ascorbic acid (0.02%) and sorbic acid (0.02%) are added to prevent the product from discoloring during cooling. The thickened finished product is poured into pre-made tin cans, sterilized and hermetically sealed. Condensed sugar-free mi Condensed sugar skimmed milk is produced from skimmed milk alone or with the addition of 20% of the rennet obtained from the production of sweet butter. Skimmed milk and butter have the same component. In terms of nutritional value, 100 grams of skimmed milk has 148-146 kJ (33-35 kcal) and 155-159 kJ (37-38 kcal) of milk. The composition of skimmed milk and ardob is given in the table below.

GENERAL TECHNOLOGY OF CEREAL PRODUCTS. FLOUR PRODUCTION TECHNOLOGY (GRAIN CLEANING

DEPARTMENT)

Flour production is the oldest industry. At first, our ancestors grinded grain between ordinary stones, then they learned to grind it in stone mills and mortars. Later, using animal, wind or water power, grain was ground (mill) using two specially prepared flat stones to produce flour. Science and technology as a result of the development of grinding machines with high production capacity (rotary cylinder machines), sorting and sieving machines (rassevs), the use of mechanical and pneumatic transport devices is being achieved. Currently, flour factories or combines in Uzbekistan are state mills each of them has the capacity to produce 250-500 tons of flour per night.

Grain processing flour production process depends on the following factors; again to the quality of processed grain; to the level of perfection of the technological process; the technical condition of the technological equipment of the enterprise; to the qualifications of specialists. According to the demand for bread products in our country: on average, each person consumes about 50 kg of bread and 165-170 kg of flour products in 1 year. And this is much higher than the indicators in other countries. The most important in the food industry and the field is the field of flour production.

Grain is an important product of agricultural production, the basis of human nutrition, and fodder base for the development of productive animal husbandry. The peculiarity of grain crops is that they contain organic substances that are extremely valuable for the human body. synthesis ability is calculated. Grain contains more dry matter than other agricultural products, which makes up 85% of the total grain mass. These are mainly high-value protein substances, digestible carbohydrates. Grains of grain contain 10...15%, and grains of legumes contain 28...30% of high-quality proteins.The share of processed grain products (flour, cereal, bread, pasta products, etc.) in human daily food ranges from 20 to 80% in different countries, on average makes 30...33%.Structure and chemical composition of wheat grain. Wheat is considered the most important food crop. It occupies the first place in the production of flour in the world. The main properties of wheat are the structure and chemical structure of the grain, as well as its organization.

The structure and composition of the tissues of the body is calculated. Physico-chemical properties of grains are evaluated by several multipliers:

a) geometrical description of grain;

b) fiber and texture of grain;

c) natural weight; g) density and size of grain;

d) weight of 1000 grains;

e) gluten formed from the protein substance of grain;

j) ash formed from grain macro- and microelements and other substances substance.

The outer layer of the grain has properties such as moisture absorption, fluidity, and dome formation. Don maccacining by xycyciyatlapi know the technological japayonlap He is excited to go. In addition, with the help of these features, it is worth considering in the processes of grinding, sieving, sorting cereals and pressing mixed feed is taken into account. Triers, ovcyug separator and The grain is separated by means of separating equipment (their models are A9-UTK-6 and A9-UTO-6). In the upper part of the hopper: a - the separating ring (ringing ring), b - the separating ring falls on sieves (grains in the nests). The size of the nests of the doll sorter is 4.5-5 mm in the working machine, 3.0-4.0 mm in the nasopat machine, and 8.0-10.0 mm in the ovsyug separator. and 9.0–11.0 mm in the control car (Figure 10). At least 75-85% of the grain waste is bran when the mill is working with high efficiency. mine waste (small stones, gravel, broken glass, metallic substances) is also cleaned in the grain mixture. Bylap cannot be separated in an air separator. If the waste gets into it, it will spoil the quality of the machine, cause it to fail or cause the machine to fail. By waste stone ajpatyv machine it is appreciated in the closing. Finally, the density of the grain is taken into account, and the dynamic coefficient of friction on the surface of the mine waste grain is calculated. The technological efficiency of BKM or BOK, BKB is 96-99%. By efficiency depends on the following factors: 100% loading of the tip, air capfi, donlapning geometric size, grain moisture, dirt, etc.Removes grain mixtures from a metal scraper magnetic yckyna and devices. A metallomagnet inside a doughnut brought to the bread making machine It can be dropped while kissing the dump, tpancpoptipovka, and moving from one area to another. In addition, as a result of the failure of the equipment in the grain cleaning shop, and in the mill, the bending of the wheels of the valet machine and it may fall during the repair of equipment in workshops. Metallomagnetic waste, in particular, when it gets into the washing and cleaning machine, causes various dangerous situations (fire). A magnetic separator is used to clean grain from magnetic debris. They work on a permanent magnet or electro-magnetic circuit. A magnetic lock that has been kicked into the block It works much better than other forms of magnetic field. The thickness of the product on the surface of the horseshoe should be 5-7 mm. The amount of magnetic sandpaper in 1 kg of fiber or coating should not exceed 0.3 mg, the size of individual particles should be larger than 0.3 mm. Flour production technology. Technological processes in flour factories are multi-system, and its separate parts are intricately connected with each other. The process of making flour from grain is divided into several stages, each of them has a certain task.

The technological process is expressed in the

form of a drawing, and their sequential execution in graphic form describes the working parameters of equipment and devices. Bread products acocan It is made from typical grains of wheat and rye. In the preparation of Makapon products, flours obtained from hard "durum" wheat or from soft, high transparency wheat is used. How many percent of flour is obtained from grains depends on the quality of the technological processes and the sequence of their number, and they are different. For example, in the production of ordinary flour, the grain is ground together with the husk and bran. Today's advanced flour This is done very easily with the help of finding technology, that is, it is done in a one-step process . In the technology of making wheat flour, the starch of the endosperm of the grain is crushed, and the starch is extracted from its shell and aleurone part. Separating the grain of grain in independent pavla it is taken and a separate product is made from it or it is also added to the product. It is difficult to isolate the endoserm in the selection method of wheat flour causes the origin of processes. Additional stages in this process are divided into different fractions according to the originality of the crushed semi-finished products, the mechanical structure of the endosperm, shell and pulp, and the physicochemical composition.

BREAD PRODUCTS PRODUCTION TECHNOLOGY

The bread industry is the most important and developed food industry is one of the fields. Year by year, the demand for bakery products is increasing and their assortment is increasing. There was no manufacturing industry in the territory of Uzbekistan until 1929. The 1st bread enterprise of our republic was built in 1929 in the city of Tashkent. In 1930, the 2nd one was built in Samarkand and the 3rd one was built in Tashkent. By 1980, the large and medium-sized bread production industry is rapidly developing in the major cities of our Republic. Main and additional raw materials are delivered to bread production enterprises in bulk in special capacities

will be brought. New technological processes are used, belt ovens, dough making units, dough folding machines and other technological equipment are installed. Bread products are baked in gas and electric ovens. The container method is used for bread transportation. The development of techniques and technologies is a working hand in 1986, the bread production enterprises were transferred from the Ministry of Food of the Republic to the Ministry of Grain Products. The production of bread, buns, macaroni, confectionery products began in the bread production enterprises. After our republic gained independence, our bread industry developed rapidly. Small enterprises with modern continuous technological lines were built instead of large-capacity old-type bread production enterprises. The advantage of small bread production enterprises is that 20-30 types of bread rolls are delivered hot to the table of residents at the same time. The range of products of the bread industry includes bread of various shapes and types, biscuits, healthy and dietary national bread products. These listed products have hundreds of names and differ from each other in their variety, shape and cooking methods. Bread products are made from rye and wheat flour of different varieties. Bread products include products weighing 0.5 kg and more. The bread is baked in special molds and on the sheets of the oven. Their recipe is simple, it includes flour, water, salt and yeast. Small amounts of sugar, fat, malt, molasses and flavoring substances are added to some types of bread. Bread products include products weighing 0.05-0.5 kg. In addition to the main raw materials, their recipe includes sugar, oil and other ingredients. Bread is the main food product. Bread is mainly a carbohydrate food, which does not meet the required optimal ratio (4:1). The nutritional value of bread depends on its calories, digestibility, amount and composition of protein, vitamins and minerals are evaluated. Nutrients contained in bread cannot be completely digested by the human body. Bread's porosity, taste, appearance, its type and other factors affect it. The higher its grade, the better its nutrients, especially protein, are digested. 1 kg of bread contains 70-80 g of protein, which covers about 30% of the human need for protein. The total amount of mineral substances in bread is 1-2%. The lower its variety, the more bread it has the amount of mineral substances will be high. Vitamins are also more abundant in them than in high quality. For example, 550g of bread made from rye and wheat will fully satisfy the human body's need for vitamin B1, vitamin B1 2.3 part, vitamin B2 satisfies 1.6 part. Organoleptic (appearance, taste, smell, core condition) and physico-chemical (moisture, acidity, porosity, fat and sugar content) quality indicators of bread and bread products are of the first level, because that the product is of poor quality according to organoleptic indicators if it is found, the product is considered unfit and further analyzes are not carried out. Bread moisture is an important indicator of its quality. Calorie content of the product, the state of the core, the amount of bread output and shelf life depends on its humidity. Moisture standards are set for each product. At present, more than 300 types of products are produced in the bread industry enterprises of the republic is being released. In recent years, in order to improve the health of the population's diet in our republic, various additives have been added to bread products, and healthy, dietary breads have been produced. is being released. These breads are prepared by adding vegetables, fruit juices, iron, proteins, bran, oat flour, rye flour, whey, enhancers and other additives. Raw materials used in the preparation of bread and bakery products are divided into two: basic and additional raw materials. The main raw materials are flour, water, yeast and salt . Additional raw materials include sugar, fat, oil, products, raw materials specified in the egg and milk recipe. Wheat flour is a powdery material obtained by grinding wheat grains in a mill. In the preparation of bread products, flours of the highest, I and II grades are used, and all types of dough are made from such flours. Its moisture is what keeps it alive It is also of great importance in the preparation of products. According to the standard, the moisture content of flour should not exceed 14.5%. All recipes for product preparation are designed for this humidity.

1. Properties of flour in baking:

2. Color of flour and change in color during bread making;
3. Rheological properties of dough, flour strength, amount and quality of gluten;
4. Its ability to absorb water;
5. Gas-forming properties of flour;
6. Its autolytic activity;

The color of the flour changes depending on the type of flour. The lower the quality of the flour, the darker its color becomes. The color of the flour is determined by the soft part of the bread.

Flour strength is a conditional term that describes the gluten content of the dough. The rheological properties of dough include: elasticity, plasticity, hardness and binding (viscosity). Based on this, flour is classified as strong, medium and weak. Strong flour contains a lot of protein. Gliadin and glutenin proteins form gluten. Water. It is the main raw material in the production of bread and pasta products. Raw water is used in the preparation of all qiyams and most confectionery masses. Drinking water is used in the preparation of food products. Enterprises are supplied with drinking water. If there is no such possibility, local water sources are used with the permission of the State Sanitary and Epidemiological Control Organizations. Regardless of the source, the water quality standard (GOST2874) must meet the requirements. It must be clear, colorless, tasteless and odorless. The amount of dissolved calcium and magnesium salts in water indicates "water hardness". Water hardness is expressed by milligram equivalents of calcium or magnesium in 1 liter of water. According to the hardness index (mg-equiv/l), water is divided into the following groups: up to 1.5 very soft; 1.5-3 soft; 3-6 slightly hard; 6-9 hard above 9 is very hard. Various water of the springs has different hardness. The hardness of drinking water can be allowed to be up to 7 mg-eq/l. Although high hardness of water has a negative effect for steam boilers, frying and other purposes, it is not harmful for making dough. Calcium and magnesium salts strengthens the properties of gluten, that is, it improves the properties of the dough made from weak flour, and the quality of the finished bread. Leavening. Pressed yeast, dried yeast, liquid in baking yeast and fermented milk are used. Yeast is a microorganism consisting of round, egg-shaped tissues belonging to the class Saccharomyces. The composition of dry fashion consists of protein 44-67%, minerals 6-8%, carbohydrates 30%, There are vitamins and enzymes. Yeast contains a number of enzymatic complexes, the main one is called zimaza. This fashion ferments the sugars in the yeast to produce ethyl alcohol and carbon dioxide (SO_2). According to this property, the dough undergoes a baking process. Favorable conditions for fermentation microorganisms are 26-28 C, 45-5 At 0C, tissue growth stops and goes into a state of anabiosis (numbness). Moisture content is 75%. The main carbohydrates for fermentation are glycogen and tregolase, which are the source of electricity. The sourness of the pressed yeast is 120-360 ml/g (in acetic acid units), the humidity is 75%, the rising power is up to 76 minutes, the yeast retains its properties at 6-8C. In production, frozen yeast is used thawed from ice (at room temperature). Pressed yeast is fed, and waste from the sugar industry is used in molasses.

Salt. Table salt is a mixture of NaCl and small amounts of other mineral salts. Table salt is divided into 4 types according to the amount of compounds in it: extra, high, type 1, type 2, iodized salt is also produced. The content of NaCl should not be less than 97-99.5%, the precipitation of dry substances insoluble in water should not exceed 0.03-0.85%, the moisture content should be 5-6% around. According to the processing method, salt is divided into fine crystalline, ground and unground salt. Type 1 and 2 of ground salt in the production of bread products is used. Salt is mainly used in the form of a 26-28% solution. Salt improves the mechanical properties of the structure of the dough and the taste of the product, reduces the activity of enzymes. At the same time, semi-finished products slow down the activity of yeast slows down the drying process. Quality indicators of salt are checked by organoleptic and physico-chemical methods.We will consider additional raw materials below. Sugar. Sugar contains 99.7% sucrose and 0.14% moisture. It dissolves completely in water, does not have an oily taste or smell, tastes sweet, and is dry to the touch. Sugar is a moisturizer because it is stored in a dry, ventilated room, the relative humidity of this room should be no more than 70%, otherwise the sugar will absorb moisture and become sticky and lumpy sugar adds flavor to bread products made from it, increases their satiety and changes the structure of the dough. Sugar inhibits gluten digestion and in this way reduces its water-holding capacity and reduces the stickiness of the dough. Dairy products. In terms of nutritional value, no product can replace milk can't. That is why milk is considered a wonderful food created by nature. Milk and milk products are easily and easily absorbed by the human body. Milk proteins consist of complete amino acids. Milk contains 2-4% casein, 0.1% globulin and 91% other proteins. Cream is obtained during the separation of milk into cream and skim milk using separators. In addition to fat, cream contains 2.5-3.4% protein, 3.0-4.2% lactose, 0.4-0.6% mineral substances are also available. The more fat it contains, the less other components it contains. The real part of the cream is sent for the production of sour cream and butter, and the cream with a fat content of 10-20% is sent for direct consumption. The fact that the cream increases in size due to the formation of foam during churning is used in the confectionery industry. The cream should be yellowish white in color. The consistency is homogeneous, fat and protein It should be without lumps, taste, and clean. The acidity of cream with 10% fat content should not exceed 19T, and the acidity of cream with 20.18 and 35% fat content should not exceed 17T. Properties of canned milk and good storage , allows them to be used directly in food, in the provision of bread, confectionery and pasta products.Dry milk and cream are prepared in two ways: thin-clay and spraying.Dry milk products include natural and skimmed dry cow's milk, dry cream, etc. Dry milk products consist of a white, yellowish powder, with a clean smell and taste characteristic of the smell and taste of pasteurized milk. The moisture content of dry milk and its products should not exceed 4-5% in hermetic packaging, and 7% in non-hermetic packaging. In the bakery and confectionery industry, whey and various products made from it are used as raw materials. Whey is a secondary product of curd and cheese production. It is a light yellow liquid with a characteristic sour taste and smell. Margarine. Margarine is basically a mixture of several types of fat, which is made by adding cream, milk or water to animal and vegetable fats. In terms of taste and smell it is close to butter. Milk and cream margarines are used in industry. Margarine for the enterprise delivered in barrels or crates. The shelf life of margarine is 45 days at a temperature of 4-10 C, 60 days at a temperature of 0-4 C and 75 days at a temperature below 0 C. The shelf life of liquid margarine is 2 days. Egg products. Eggs are a very nutritious, energetic food, which contains proteins, fats, minerals and other substances. Eggs awaken the taste of products with their properties, making them fluffy and flawless. Egg white has astringent properties, creates a good foam and holds juice. Malt and malt preparations. Malt under artificial conditions at a certain temperature and humidity levied grain.

The process of harvesting grain artificially is called malting. The harvested product is called Fresh Malt and it is then dried and converted into Dry Malt. Barley and rye grain are mainly used for making malt. Dried fermented (red) and unfermented (white) rye from rye grain. malt, and barley is used to make white and black, caramelized and charred barley malt, which is used to make beer. In baking, it mainly uses fermented (red) and unfermented (white) rye malt. Starch and feed products. Starch is the main reserve substance that accumulates in the seeds, pods or roots of plants. Its chemical composition is starch polysaccharide, the basis of its structure is glucose residues. Therefore, starch is broken down into hydrolyzed glucose and is almost completely absorbed by the body. A person's daily need for starch is 400-500g. The amount of starch that enters the body with food is half of the energy requirement of a person Satisfies. Edible fats and oils. Vegetable oils and fats obtained from animal tissues are usually not chemically pure. They are very complex mixtures in which oils are the main component and other components are mixtures of oils or fatty substances. Plant lipids are mainly collected in fruits and seeds. In animals and fish, fat accumulates in subcutaneous tissues surrounding vital organs. Depending on the source of the oil, vegetable, animal and combined oils are liquid depending on their consistency. Combined fats are fats obtained by mixing animal, vegetable and hydrated fats. These are margarine, cooking and special oils.

The production of bread and bakery products consists of the following six main stages:

1. Reception and storage of raw materials;
2. Preparation of raw materials for commissioning;
3. Preparation of dough;
4. Divide the dough;
5. Cooking;
6. Storage of the cooked product and sending it for sale;

The first stage - covers the reception and storage of raw materials in dry or molten state coming to enterprises in warehouses and containers under certain conditions. Flour is brought to the bakery in flour transport machines equipped with compressors and is taken to special silos. Here the flour is stored and made for 7 days. Other raw materials, such as salt, are brought to small bakeries whole, melted in special three-section tanks, cooled for a certain period, filtered and stored in liquid form. The concentration of salt solution should be -26% density -1.19 g/l. Pressed yeasts are brought in boxes and stored in freezers for 3 days at a temperature of 0-4C. Sugar is delivered to the bakery dry in bags and density 1, 2, 3 is brought in melted and heated cisterns. Then it is poured into stainless steel containers and stored in a solution state. and is brought in containers with a heating coating that maintains a certain level. The second stage is the preparation of raw materials for production.

The stored flour is passed through the "Vinklar" brand sifter, which consists of a sieve and a magnet, which removes various impurities and metal particles. To increase fermentation, the broth is prepared in special containers and raised for 1-2 hours at a temperature of 30C. Sugar production is stopped. The remaining raw materials are also washed and cleaned and brought to production.

The third stage is preparation of dough. Dough preparation is an important process in the production of bread products, and the next technological stages and the quality of bread directly depend on this process. The main purpose of the dough is a certain amount of flour consists of mixing water, yeast, salt and other components to form a mixture of the same composition. The process of dough preparation is carried out in a "Winkler" dough mixing machine. Water for kneading the dough through the dispenser to the deja (dough kneading pot) is transmitted. The remaining raw materials are covered with specially sized buckets. The dough is intensively mixed for 10 minutes. When preparing dough, we try to create good conditions for it to rise. Dough is added to make sweet-tasting, well-porous bread. Dough is raised in three different ways: biochemical, chemical and mechanical methods. Biochemically, yeasts are added to the dough, which break down the sugars contained in the dough into alcohol and carbon IV oxide.Chemically, baking soda, ammonium carbonate salt, etc. are added to the dough additions are added. During cooking, they break down under the influence of high temperature and form carbon IV-oxide, which increases the dough. In the mechanical method, the dough is kept under the pressure of carbon IV-oxide gas in a special device. In this process, the porous dough mass is shaped and sent for baking.

The fourth stage is the process of dividing the dough, and it includes the processes of folding the dough, giving it a shape and letting it rest for a certain period of time. The MAK-3 dough dividing machine of the company "Winkler" gives the dough to the dough balls of the specified weight. The weight of the dough is determined based on the weight of the finished product, which takes into account the weight loss of bread products during baking. Some bread products are shaped in special devices. Formed pieces of dough are kneaded, while the dough continues to rise the resulting gas makes the dough porous and increases its size. Asking 35-40C temperature and 75-85% relative humidity are favorable conditions for the process. The search process is carried out in special cameras.

The fifth stage is the baking process, in which the dough turns into a finished bread product. The purpose of cooking is to turn the dough into a digestible product consists of The purpose of cooking is to turn the dough into a digestible product consists of In the first few minutes of the cooking process, it can be observed that it rises by a certain amount. This process occurs through the penetration of heat between the layers of dough. At the initial time of temperature increase in the inner layers of the brain, it causes the formation of a large amount of carbon dioxide gas by yeasts. When the temperature reaches 55 C, the activity of yeast stops. The upper part of the dough pieces heats up quickly in the oven, and the fermenting microorganisms in this layer die immediately, the starch grains are clustered, and the proteins are denatured. When the temperature reaches 1000C, moisture starts to evaporate from the dough. It is explained by the hardening of the upper part, the evaporation of a large amount of moisture in it. Discoloration of the upper part, it is chemical it is the result of the processes taking place. As the temperature of the dough increases, strins are formed from pasteurized starch, for example, light yellow dextrins are formed at 110-1200C, brown dextrins are formed at 120-1400C. Caramelization process of sugars occurs when the temperature is 140-1500C. occurs. At 150-2000C, dark colored substances - melanoids are formed as a result of the interaction of proteins and sugars in the upper part of the bread. Melanoids are substances that give the taste and aroma specific to bread prod because it is a poor conductor of heat. Even if the cooking time is extended, the temperature of the bread core does not exceed 100ºC. After the temperature reaches 60ºC, the process of deaturation of proteins (svertvania) begins. In this case, water is released from the protein molecule, and the water is the starch that is pasteurized binds. Thus, due to the baking process, a bread core is formed, which has a strong framework consisting of starch granules and proteins whose structure has changed. The alcohol formed as a result of chemical changes reacts with the acids in the dough and turns into esters that give the bread a pleasant taste and aroma. The cooking mode is determined for each type of bread products, which is the duration of cooking and characterized by the relative humidity in the chamber. The taste and aroma of the bread depends primarily on the duration of cooking and the speed of heating the dough in the oven. The duration of cooking depends on the weight and shape of the products, the temperature regime, the density of the dough pieces and other factors. takes Baked in the oven, the bread is transferred to the circulation tables through belt conveyors, from where the loaves are placed on wooden trays. These trays are movable and gonekas is located, bread storage until the bread products in the vans are sent to the trade networks stored in warehouses. Requirements for packaging, storage and shipping of bakery products are defined in standard norms. The period of storage of manufactured bread products in the enterprise is determined, in which it is important to keep bread fresh. The storage period lasts from the time it comes out of the oven until it is sent to Issik Non stores. Bread products that have passed their shelf life in a factory or store are considered waste and are processed to obtain products such as talc, sukhari flour. The weight loss is determined by the difference between the weights of the hot bread and the cooled bread.This process continues until the relative humidity of the surrounding air is balanced. Depending on the type of product and the conditions of storage, weight loss in bread products is 1-3%. During storage, the upper part of the bread hardens. After a few hours of baking, the tops of the bread are soft from a firm, crumbly state becomes elastic. The masculinity of the bread dough decreases, the friction increases. This process, the products of which are kept at a temperature of 0-250C, is intensive. Lowering the temperature to 70C slows down this process. Keeping bread products fresh is important. Due to the fact that bread production enterprises work continuously day and night bakery products prepared in the evening shift reach customers after 10-12 hours. Therefore, to keep them fresh, they are packed in polyethylene bags nowadays is being widely implemented. Polyethylene package preserves the freshness, taste, aroma and softness of bread for 2-3 days helps to keep well during. Packaging materials for bread products should have certain durability, be inert, harmless to products.

Production technology of pasta products

Pasta products have been produced since ancient times: first in the form of flat noodles, and later in the form of tubular pasta. The first description of how to prepare ugra can be found in the culinary treatise of Anicho, a Roman culinary expert, compiled in the first decade of the new era. Documentary records of pasta cooking in Italy date back to the beginning of the 12th century. Until the middle of the 14th century, pasta products were prepared at home. The first pasta production shops with simple techniques were built in Italy at the end of the 14th century. Macaroni and vermicelli are pressed in screw-type wooden presses and dried in frames on racks installed in the workshop building. The next big step in the pasta industry was the introduction of non-stop dryers, and based on them, mechanized lines in the unit of screw presses appeared: in 1945-1948, the first lines of the company "Braybanti" (Italy) for the production of short products, 50- the first lines of the Buhler company (Switzerland) for the production of long products at the beginning of the years. The further development of the pasta industry, which continues until now, is on the path of modernizing the techniques and technologies of dough kneading and shaping, drying of pasta products, and expanding the assortment (varieties) of products. In this sense, it is necessary to emphasize the use of vacuum processing of the dough, the use of matrices with Teflon additives, the use of high-temperature drying mode, and the use of technological methods for the production of fast-cooking products.

Currently, Italy is in the first place in terms of production, consumption and export of pasta products: in the last decade, the average annual production of pasta products in Italy varies from 1800 to 2500 thousand tons. Pasta The USA ranks second in the production of its products: 1300-1800 thousand tons per year. As for the equipment used for the production of pasta products, Italy is at the forefront here. Two ancient Italian firms: "Braybanti" and "Pavon" - produce the most modernized lines for the production of long, short and honeycomb pasta products, which are widely used in almost all countries of the world. Only the lines of the Swiss "Bühler" company are competitive to them.

Pasta, a staple food in many cultures, is cherished for its versatility, nutritional value, and ease of preparation. From traditional spaghetti and penne to innovative gluten-free and whole grain varieties, the technology behind pasta production has evolved significantly. This article delves into the intricacies of pasta production technology, highlighting the processes, equipment, and innovations that contribute to making this beloved food.Raw MaterialsThe primary ingredient in pasta is durum wheat semolina, valued for its high protein content and gluten strength, which give pasta its firm texture. Other types of flour, such as whole wheat, rice, corn, and quinoa, are used to produce various pasta types catering to dietary needs and preferences. Eggs, water, and sometimes additional ingredients like spinach or tomato puree are incorporated to create different pasta flavors and colors.Production ProcessMixing and KneadingBlending: The process begins with blending the semolina or flour with water (and eggs, if used). Precise measurement is crucial to achieve the desired dough consistency.Kneading: The mixture is kneaded to develop gluten, forming a dough that is elastic and pliable.ExtrusionExtrusion Process: The dough is pushed through dies to shape the pasta. These dies come in various shapes and sizes, allowing the production of diverse pasta forms such as spaghetti, fusilli, and macaroni.Vacuum Extrusion: Modern extrusion processes often use vacuum technology to remove air bubbles, enhancing the pasta's texture and appearance.DryingInitial Drying: The extruded pasta undergoes pre-drying to reduce surface moisture, preventing stickiness.Main Drying: The pasta is then dried in controlled environments with specific temperature and humidity settings. This step is critical as it affects the final product's quality, shelf life, and cooking properties.Cooling: After drying, the pasta is gradually cooled to room temperature to avoid cracks and fractures.Cutting and PackagingCutting: For certain pasta types, such as lasagna or tagliatelle, the dried pasta is cut into the desired lengths and shapes.Packaging: The final product is packaged in various forms, such as boxes, bags, or vacuum-sealed containers, ensuring protection and extended shelf life.Innovations in Pasta ProductionGluten-Free PastaInnovations in using alternative flours like rice, corn, and quinoa have made it possible to produce high-quality gluten-free pasta. Advanced blending techniques and additives ensure that these pasta varieties maintain desirable texture and cooking properties.Whole Grain and High-Protein PastaWith the growing demand for healthier options, pasta made from whole grains and legumes like chickpeas and lentils has become popular. These varieties offer higher fiber and protein content, catering to health-conscious consumers.Automation and RoboticsModern pasta factories employ automated systems and robotics for mixing, extrusion, drying, and packaging. These technologies enhance production efficiency, consistency, and hygiene.Sustainability PracticesSustainability is a key focus in contemporary pasta production. Innovations include using energy-efficient drying methods, biodegradable packaging materials, and sustainable sourcing of raw materials to reduce the environmental impact.Quality ControlMaintaining high quality is crucial in pasta production. Quality control measures include:Moisture Content: Ensuring the correct moisture level to avoid spoilage and ensure optimal texture.Texture and Taste: Regular sensory evaluations to maintain the desired pasta characteristics.Microbial Safety: Routine testing for contaminants to ensure food safety standards are met.Pasta production technology has advanced remarkably, blending traditional methods with modern innovations to meet the evolving demands of consumers. From the careful selection of raw materials to the precision of extrusion and drying processes, each step is integral to producing high-quality pasta. As technology continues to evolve, the pasta industry is poised to deliver even more diverse, nutritious, and sustainable products to satisfy global appetites.

CLASSIFICATION OF PASTA PRODUCTS: A COMPREHENSIVE GUIDE

Pasta is a beloved staple in many cuisines around the world, renowned for its versatility, ease of preparation, and ability to pair well with a wide range of ingredients and sauces. This article explores the various classifications of pasta products, focusing on shape, ingredients, and intended culinary use.Classification by ShapePasta comes in numerous shapes and sizes, each designed to enhance different types of dishes. Here's a look at the major categories:Long PastaSpaghetti: Thin, cylindrical strands, ideal for a wide variety of sauces, from marinara to carbonara.Linguine: Slightly flattened spaghetti, perfect for seafood dishes like linguine alle vongole.Fettuccine: Flat, thick noodles often paired with rich, creamy sauces like Alfredo.Angel Hair (Capellini): Very thin strands, best suited for light sauces or broths.Short PastaPenne: Tube-shaped with diagonal cuts, suitable for baked dishes and thick, hearty sauces.Fusilli: Spiral-shaped pasta that holds onto thick sauces well.Macaroni: Small, curved tubes, commonly used in macaroni and cheese.Farfalle: Bow-tie shaped, versatile for both hot dishes and pasta salads.Soup PastaOrzo: Rice-shaped pasta, commonly used in soups and salads.Ditalini: Small, short tubes perfect for minestrone and other hearty soups.Pastina: Tiny shapes like stars or rings, often used in light soups for children.

Stuffed PastaRavioli: Square or circular pasta filled with cheese, meat, or vegetables.Tortellini: Ring-shaped pasta stuffed similarly to ravioli, often served in broth.Cannelloni: Large tubes filled with ricotta and spinach or meat, then baked.Sheet PastaLasagna: Wide, flat sheets used in layered baked dishes with sauce, cheese, and meat or vegetables.

Classification by IngredientsThe ingredients used in pasta can significantly influence its texture, flavor, and nutritional value.

Traditional PastaMade from durum wheat

semolina and water, known for its firm texture and yellow color.

Egg Pasta Includes eggs in the dough, giving it a richer flavor and a more tender texture. Common in fettuccine and tagliatelle.

Whole Grain PastaMade from whole wheat flour, offering higher fiber content and a nuttier flavor. A healthier alternative to traditional pasta.

Gluten-Free PastaMade from alternative flours such as rice, corn, quinoa, or legume-based flours like chickpeas and lentils. Suitable for those with gluten intolerance or celiac disease.

Vegetable-Enriched Pasta Incorporates vegetable purees like spinach, tomato, or beetroot, adding color, flavor, and nutritional value.

Classification by Intended UsePasta can also be classified based on how it is used or prepared in culinary applications.

Dry PastaThe most common type, sold in packages and can be stored for long periods. Requires boiling before use. Ideal for a wide range of dishes.

Fresh PastaMade with fresh ingredients and has a shorter shelf life. Offers a tender texture and is often used in gourmet dishes. Requires shorter cooking time than dry pasta.

Frozen PastaOften pre-cooked and frozen. Convenient for quick meals and maintains good texture upon reheating.Instant PastaPre-cooked and dried, requiring minimal cooking time. Often found in instant meal kits and convenient for quick preparations.Special VarietiesOrganic PastaMade from organically grown ingredients without synthetic pesticides or fertilizers. Appeals to health-conscious consumers.High-Protein PastaEnhanced with additional protein sources like legumes or added protein powders. Targets athletes and those seeking higher protein intake.Flavored PastaInfused with additional flavors such as garlic, herb, or truffle. Adds a gourmet touch to dishes.

The classification of pasta products is vast and varied, reflecting its global popularity and culinary versatility. From the familiar shapes of spaghetti and penne to innovative gluten-free and high-protein varieties, each type of pasta brings its unique characteristics to the table.

Understanding these classifications not only enriches the culinary experience but also allows for more informed choices to suit dietary needs and preferences. Whether enjoyed in a simple aglio e olio or a complex lasagna, pasta remains a beloved food that continues to evolve and delight palates worldwide.

Description of the Main Stages in the Preparation of Pasta Products

Pasta, a culinary staple enjoyed globally, undergoes a series of well-defined stages in its preparation. From selecting the finest raw materials to the final packaging, each step is crucial to ensure the pasta's quality, texture, and flavor. This article provides an in-depth look at the main stages involved in the preparation of pasta products.

1. Selection of Raw MaterialsThe foundation of high-quality pasta lies in the selection of superior raw materials.Durum Wheat Semolina: The primary ingredient, chosen for its high protein content and strong gluten, which provides the desired firmness and elasticity in pasta.Water: Essential for forming the dough, the quality of

water can impact the pasta's final texture.Additional Ingredients: Depending on the type of pasta, additional ingredients such as eggs, vegetable purees (like spinach or tomato), or alternative flours (for gluten-free varieties) may be used.

2. Mixing and KneadingThe process begins with combining the raw materials to form a homogeneous dough.Blending: Durum wheat semolina or flour is mixed with water (and eggs, if used) in precise proportions to achieve the correct dough consistency.Kneading: The mixture is then kneaded to develop gluten, giving the dough its elastic properties. This step is crucial for ensuring the pasta's ability to hold its shape during cooking.

3. Extrusion or RollingThe dough is then shaped into various pasta forms through extrusion or rolling.Extrusion: The dough is pushed through molds or dies to create different shapes like spaghetti, penne, and fusilli. The choice of die determines the pasta's final form. Modern extruders often use vacuum technology to remove air bubbles, resulting in a smoother texture.Rolling and Cutting: For flat pasta types

such as lasagna or fettuccine, the dough is rolled out into thin sheets and then cut into the desired shape and size.

4. DryingDrying is a critical stage that affects the pasta's shelf life, texture, and cooking properties.Pre-Drying: The freshly shaped pasta undergoes pre-drying to reduce surface moisture. This helps prevent the pasta from sticking together.Main Drying: The pasta is then dried in controlled environments with specific temperature and humidity settings. This process can take from several hours to days, depending on the pasta type. Proper drying ensures that the pasta maintains its shape and texture during cooking.Cooling: After drying, the pasta is gradually cooled to room temperature to prevent cracks and fractures.

5. Quality ControlEnsuring consistent quality throughout the production process is essential.Moisture Content: Regular checks are conducted to ensure the pasta has the correct moisture content, which is vital for shelf stability.Texture and Taste: Sensory evaluations are performed to ensure the pasta meets the desired standards for texture and flavor.Microbial Safety: Routine testing for contaminants and

pathogens is conducted to ensure the pasta is safe for consumption.

6. Cutting and ShapingFor certain pasta types, additional cutting and shaping are required after drying.Cutting: Dried pasta sheets are cut into specific shapes and sizes, such as lasagna sheets or tagliatelle strands.Shaping: Some pasta types, like tortellini or ravioli, require further shaping and filling after the initial drying stage.

7. PackagingPackaging protects the pasta and extends its shelf life while providing important information to consumers.Packaging Materials: Pasta is packaged in various forms such as boxes, bags, or vacuum-sealed containers, each offering different levels of protection and shelf life extension.Labeling: Packages are labeled with nutritional information, cooking instructions, and expiration dates. Branding and design also play a significant role in appealing to consumers.The preparation of pasta products involves a meticulous process that ensures the final product is of high quality and meets consumer expectations. From selecting the best raw materials to careful drying and packaging, each stage is integral to producing pasta that is

delicious, nutritious, and safe. Understanding these stages highlights the craftsmanship and technology behind one of the world's most beloved foods.

Making Pasta Dough

Pasta dough is the foundation of countless beloved dishes, from simple spaghetti to sophisticated ravioli. Mastering the art of making pasta dough is both an essential skill for home cooks and a fascinating journey into the heart of Italian cuisine. This article provides a detailed guide to making perfect pasta dough, covering traditional methods, ingredients, and tips for success.IngredientsThe beauty of pasta dough lies in its simplicity. The basic ingredients are few, but their quality and proportions are crucial.FlourDurum Wheat Semolina: Preferred for its high gluten content, providing the pasta with a firm texture and yellow hue.All-Purpose Flour: Often used in combination with semolina for a softer dough.00 Flour: A finely milled Italian flour, excellent for making tender, delicate pasta.EggsFresh, high-quality eggs contribute to the dough's richness and color. The traditional ratio is one egg per 100 grams of flour.WaterUsed sparingly, usually when making pasta without eggs, like certain regional Italian varieties.SaltA pinch of salt enhances the dough's flavor, although it is optional as the pasta can absorb seasoning from the cooking water and sauce.Olive Oil (Optional)A small amount can be added to the dough for extra elasticity and flavor, though traditional recipes often omit it.EquipmentWhile pasta dough can be made entirely by hand, a few tools can make the process easier.Mixing BowlFor combining the ingredients.Fork or Dough ScraperFor initial mixing and kneading.Pasta MachineFor rolling out and cutting the dough, though a rolling pin and knife can also be used.Plastic WrapFor resting the dough.Step-by-Step Guide1. Measuring and MixingStart by measuring out your ingredients accurately. For a basic egg pasta dough, the typical ratio is 100 grams of flour per egg.

Step 1: Pour the flour into a mound on a clean work surface or in a large mixing bowl

.Step 2: Create a well in the center of the flour.

Step 3: Crack the eggs into the well and add a pinch of salt (if using).2. Incorporating the

Ingredients

Step 4: Using a fork, gently beat the eggs, gradually incorporating the flour from the edges of the well.

Step 5: Continue mixing until a shaggy dough begins to form.3. Kneading the Dough

Step 6: Use your hands to bring the dough together and start kneading.

Step 7: Knead the dough for about 10 minutes. It should become smooth, elastic, and slightly tacky but not sticky. If the dough is too dry, add a few drops of water. If it's too wet, sprinkle with a bit more flour.4. Resting the Dough

Step 8: Shape the dough into a ball and wrap it tightly in plastic wrap.

Step 9: Let the dough rest at room temperature for at least 30 minutes. This relaxes the gluten, making the dough easier to roll out.5. Rolling Out the DoughIf using a pasta machine

Step 10: Divide the dough into smaller portions to make it more manageable.

Step 11: Flatten one portion with your hands and

pass it through the widest setting of the pasta machine.

Step 12: Fold the dough into thirds and pass it through the machine again. Repeat this process several times to develop the dough's structure.

Step 13: Gradually reduce the machine's thickness setting, passing the dough through each setting until you reach the desired thickness.If rolling by hand

Step 14: On a lightly floured surface, roll out the dough with a rolling pin, rotating it frequently to ensure even thickness.6. Cutting the Dough

Step 15: Once rolled out, the dough can be cut into various shapes. Use a knife or the cutting attachment on your pasta machine for fettuccine, tagliatelle, or other shapes.Tips for SuccessQuality Ingredients: Use the best quality flour and eggs you can find.Kneading: Proper kneading is crucial for gluten development, which gives pasta its structure.Resting: Don't skip the resting period. It makes rolling out the dough much easier.Consistency: Adjust flour or water as needed to achieve the right dough consistency. It should be smooth and elastic.ConclusionMaking pasta dough from scratch is a rewarding process that connects you to centuries of culinary tradition. With just a few simple ingredients and a bit of practice, you can create delicious, homemade pasta that far surpasses store-bought varieties in flavor and texture. Whether you're making a humble spaghetti or an elaborate filled pasta, understanding the fundamentals of pasta dough is the first step to culinary mastery.

Pressing Pasta Dough: A Key Step in Pasta Production

Pressing pasta dough is a critical step in the pasta-making process, particularly when using a pasta machine or extruder. This step transforms the dough into thin sheets or various shapes, preparing it for cooking or drying. Understanding the pressing process can help ensure the final pasta product has the desired texture, thickness, and consistency. This article explores the pressing stage in detail, including methods, equipment, and tips for success.The Importance of PressingPressing the pasta dough properly ensures:Uniform Thickness: Achieving consistent thickness across the dough sheet, which is essential for even cooking.Smooth Texture:

Producing a smooth and elastic dough surface that enhances the pasta's quality.Shape and Form: Enabling the dough to be shaped into various pasta types, from flat sheets to intricate shapes like fusilli or macaroni.Equipment for Pressing Pasta DoughPasta MachineA common tool for home cooks and small-scale production. It consists of rollers that press the dough into thin sheets and cutters for shaping.ExtruderUsed in both artisanal and industrial settings, this machine forces the dough through dies to create specific shapes. It is ideal for making tubular or complex pasta shapes.Rolling PinA manual tool for pressing dough, useful for traditional or smaller batches. Requires more effort and skill to achieve uniform thickness.Steps in Pressing Pasta Dough1. Preparing the DoughBefore pressing, the dough must be properly prepared:Kneading: Ensure the dough is smooth and elastic, having been kneaded thoroughly.Resting: Allow the dough to rest, covered, for at least 30 minutes to relax the gluten. This makes it easier to roll out and press.2. Dividing the DoughPortioning: Divide the dough into smaller, manageable portions. This prevents overworking and ensures even pressing.Flattening: Lightly flatten each portion with your hands before feeding it into the machine.3. Using a Pasta MachineInitial Passes: Set the pasta machine to the widest setting. Pass the dough through the rollers, then fold it into thirds and pass it through again. Repeat this process several times to build the dough's structure.Gradual Rolling: Gradually narrow the setting on the machine with each pass, reducing the thickness incrementally. Typically, you'll pass the dough through 4-5 settings until it reaches the desired thickness.Consistency Check: Ensure the dough is not too sticky or dry. Lightly dust with flour if it sticks, but avoid over-flouring, which can dry out the dough.4. Using an ExtruderLoading the Extruder: Load the kneaded and rested dough into the extruder.Selecting Dies: Choose the appropriate die for the pasta shape you want to create.Extrusion Process: Turn on the extruder and allow the dough to be pushed through the die, forming the desired shapes.Cutting: As the pasta emerges, use a cutter or knife to trim it to the appropriate length.5. Manual Rolling with a Rolling PinRolling Out: Place the dough on a lightly floured surface. Roll from the center outward, rotating the dough frequently to ensure even thickness.Achieving Thinness: Continue rolling until the dough is uniformly thin, as specified for the pasta type you are making.Tips for Successful PressingDough Consistency: Ensure the dough is well-kneaded and rested. It should be smooth and slightly elastic.Even Pressure: Apply consistent pressure when using a rolling pin or feeding dough into a machine to achieve even thickness.Dusting: Use flour sparingly to prevent sticking, but avoid over-dusting, which can alter the dough's texture.Patience: Don't rush the pressing process. Gradually reduce the thickness to maintain the dough's integrity.Troubleshooting Common IssuesSticky Dough: If the dough sticks to the rollers or extruder, dust it lightly with flour. If it's too sticky, it might need more kneading.Tearing or Breaking: If the dough tears, it may be too dry or not sufficiently kneaded. Add a bit of water and knead again before resting.Uneven Thickness: Ensure you are not skipping settings on the pasta machine and that the dough is consistently flattened before each pass.ConclusionPressing pasta dough is a crucial step that transforms raw ingredients into beautiful, uniformly shaped pasta. Whether using a pasta machine, extruder, or rolling pin, mastering this step ensures your pasta will cook evenly and have the desired texture and appearance. By paying attention to dough consistency, equipment settings, and technique, you can achieve perfect pasta every time, ready to be paired with your favorite sauces and ingredients.

Technology of Drying and Cooling Pasta Products

Drying and cooling are critical stages in the production of pasta products, significantly affecting their quality, shelf life, and cooking properties. These processes must be carefully controlled to ensure the final product maintains its desired texture, flavor, and nutritional value. This article explores the technology and methods used in the drying and cooling of pasta products.Importance of DryingDrying pasta serves several essential purposes:Preservation: Reduces moisture content to prevent microbial growth and extend shelf life.Texture: Ensures the pasta retains its shape and firmness during cooking.Storage: Facilitates safe long-term storage without refrigeration.Drying TechnologyPre-DryingPurpose: To reduce surface moisture and prevent pasta pieces from sticking together.Method: Pasta is subjected to a short period of warm, dry air circulation immediately after shaping.Equipment: Pre-drying tunnels or chambers with controlled temperature and airflow.Main DryingPurpose: To reduce the pasta's internal moisture content to a safe level (typically below 12%).Stages:Initial Drying: Involves higher temperatures to quickly reduce moisture.Intermediate Drying: Uses moderate temperatures to ensure even moisture removal.Final Drying: Low temperatures for a prolonged period to achieve the desired moisture level without causing cracks or defects.Method: Controlled environment drying with precise regulation of temperature, humidity, and airflow.Equipment:Static Dryers: Traditional method where pasta is spread on trays in a drying chamber.Continuous Dryers: Modern method where pasta moves through drying zones on conveyor belts.Vacuum Dryers: Used for delicate pasta shapes to dry at lower temperatures and reduce the risk of deformation.Factors Influencing DryingTemperature: Higher temperatures speed up drying but can cause surface hardening or cracks if not carefully controlled.Humidity: Controlled humidity prevents rapid drying, which can lead to structural damage.Airflow: Adequate circulation ensures even drying across all pasta pieces.Time: Drying time varies depending on the pasta shape, size, and moisture content.Cooling TechnologyPurpose of CoolingTo stabilize the pasta after drying and prevent moisture condensation when packaged.To ensure the pasta reaches room temperature gradually to avoid thermal shocks that can cause cracks.Cooling StagesInitial Cooling: Gradual reduction of temperature immediately after drying.Final Cooling: Bringing pasta to room temperature in a controlled environment.Methods and EquipmentCooling Tunnels: Enclosed systems with controlled airflow and temperature settings.Ambient Cooling: Allowing pasta to cool naturally in a controlled environment, often used for smaller batches.Forced Air Cooling: Using fans or air conditioners to circulate air and reduce temperature quickly.Modern Innovations in Drying and CoolingEnergy EfficiencyHeat Recovery Systems: Capturing and reusing heat from drying processes to reduce energy consumption.Optimized Airflow Designs: Improving air circulation patterns to enhance drying efficiency.Automation and

Control Advanced Sensors: Monitoring temperature, humidity, and moisture content in real-time. Computerized Control Systems: Automatically adjusting drying parameters to maintain optimal conditions. Programmable Logic Controllers (PLCs): For precise control over drying and cooling cycles, ensuring consistent quality. Sustainability Eco-Friendly Materials: Using biodegradable or recyclable materials in drying and cooling equipment. Waste Reduction: Minimizing waste through efficient process control and reduced energy consumption. Best Practices for Drying and Cooling Consistent Monitoring Regularly check and calibrate equipment to ensure optimal performance. Monitor moisture content at different stages to prevent under- or over-drying. Maintenance Routine maintenance of dryers and coolers to avoid breakdowns and ensure efficiency. Clean equipment regularly to prevent contamination and ensure hygienic processing conditions. Quality Control Conduct regular quality checks to ensure the pasta meets desired standards for moisture content, texture, and appearance. Test samples from different batches to maintain consistency and detect any issues early.The technology of drying and cooling pasta products is crucial for producing high-quality pasta with a long shelf life and excellent cooking properties. By utilizing advanced equipment and maintaining precise control over environmental conditions, manufacturers can ensure their pasta products meet consumer expectations and regulatory standards. Understanding and implementing these technologies effectively is key to the success of any pasta production operation.

Packaging Technology of Pasta Products

Packaging plays a crucial role in the pasta production process, ensuring that the product remains safe, fresh, and appealing to consumers. The technology behind pasta packaging has evolved significantly, focusing on materials, machinery, and methods that enhance the product's shelf life, ease of use, and environmental sustainability. This article delves into the various technologies and practices used in the packaging of pasta products.Functions of Pasta PackagingProtection: Shields the pasta from physical damage, moisture, and contamination.Preservation: Maintains freshness by preventing exposure to air and humidity.Information: Provides essential details like nutritional information, cooking instructions, and expiry dates.Convenience: Offers easy-to-open, resealable, and portion-controlled options.Branding: Enhances visual appeal and communicates brand identity to consumers.Types of Packaging MaterialsPlastic:Polyethylene (PE): Widely used for its flexibility and moisture barrier properties.Polypropylene (PP): Offers higher temperature resistance, making it suitable for microwaveable packaging.Polyethylene Terephthalate (PET): Common for clear, rigid containers that showcase the product.Paper and Cardboard:Corrugated Boxes: Often used for bulk packaging and transportation.Cartons: Provide rigidity and protection while being easily printable for branding.Composite Materials:Laminates: Combine multiple materials to leverage their collective benefits, such as barrier properties of aluminum foil with the flexibility of plastic films.Biodegradable and Recyclable Materials:PLA (Polylactic Acid): Derived from renewable resources like corn starch, offering an eco-friendly alternative.Recycled Paper: Used increasingly to reduce environmental impact.Packaging Types and FormatsFlexible Packaging:Bags and Pouches: Common for dry pasta, often with resealable options to maintain freshness.Stand-Up Pouches: Offer convenience and improved shelf presence.Rigid Packaging:Boxes and Cartons: Provide sturdy protection and ample space for branding and information.Jars and Tubs: Typically used for specialty pasta or fresh pasta that requires refrigeration.Bulk Packaging:Large Bags or Sacks: Used for commercial or industrial distribution.Palletized Containers: Facilitate easy transport and storage in large quantities.Packaging Machinery and ProcessesForm-Fill-Seal (FFS) Machines:Vertical FFS: Suitable for bagging dry pasta, forming bags from a flat roll of film, filling them with pasta, and sealing them.Horizontal FFS: Used for more delicate pasta shapes or prepared pasta products.Cartoning Machines:Automatically erect, fill, and close cartons, providing efficiency and consistency for boxed pasta products.Flow Wrapping Machines:Encase pasta in a continuous film, creating a sealed package that is cut into individual units.Weighing and Dispensing Systems:Ensure accurate portion control and consistent filling, crucial for maintaining product weight standards. Vacuum Packaging: Removes air from the package to extend shelf life, particularly useful for fresh or refrigerated pasta. Modified Atmosphere Packaging (MAP): Replaces the air inside the package with a specific gas mixture (usually nitrogen or carbon dioxide) to prolong freshness and prevent spoilage. Sustainability in Pasta Packaging Material Reduction: Using thinner films or lighter materials to reduce the environmental footprint without compromising protection. Recyclable and Biodegradable Options: Increasing use of materials that can be easily recycled or that biodegrade naturally, reducing waste. Eco-Friendly Practices: Adopting practices such as using renewable energy in packaging plants and optimizing packaging designs to reduce material usage and transportation impact. Innovations in Packaging Technology Smart Packaging: Incorporating QR codes or RFID tags to provide consumers with additional information, such as traceability, cooking tips, and promotional content. Active Packaging: Integrating materials that actively interact with the product to enhance preservation, such as moisture absorbers or antimicrobial agents.Customizable Packaging:Flexible designs that allow for personalization and seasonal variations, enhancing consumer engagement.ConclusionThe technology of pasta packaging has advanced significantly, integrating sophisticated materials and machinery to ensure product safety, freshness, and appeal. With growing emphasis on sustainability and innovation, the future of pasta packaging will likely see even more eco-friendly materials, smart packaging solutions, and consumer-focused designs. By understanding and leveraging these technologies, manufacturers can continue to meet consumer demands while minimizing environmental impact.

Technology of Production of Meat Products: SausageIntroductionSausage production is a complex process that involves various stages, from meat selection to packaging. Modern sausage production technology ensures that the final product is safe, flavorful, and consistent in quality. This article explores the technology and methods used in sausage production, covering each stage in detail.1. Selection and Preparation of Raw MaterialsThe quality of sausages starts with the selection of raw materials.Meat Selection:

Typically includes pork, beef, or a combination. Poultry and game meats are also used. The quality and cut of meat significantly affect the sausage's final texture and flavor.Fat: Added to improve flavor, juiciness, and texture. Commonly used fats include pork fatback or beef tallow.Non-Meat Ingredients: Include water, salt, curing agents (like sodium nitrite), spices, and seasonings. Fillers such as breadcrumbs or soy protein may also be used in some recipes.2. Meat Grinding and MixingOnce the raw materials are selected, they are processed to create the sausage mixture.Grinding: The meat and fat are ground to a specific consistency using a meat grinder. The grind size can vary depending on the type of sausage being produced.Mixing: The ground meat is mixed with spices, seasonings, and other ingredients. This can be done manually or using industrial mixers to ensure a homogeneous blend. For some sausages, ice or cold water is added during mixing to maintain a low temperature, which is crucial for texture and safety.3. Emulsification (for certain types of sausages)Purpose: To create a fine-textured product, such as hot dogs or bologna.Process: The meat mixture is finely chopped and blended in a bowl chopper or emulsifier, creating a smooth paste.4. StuffingThe mixed or emulsified meat is then stuffed into casings.Casings: Can be natural (made from animal intestines), collagen, cellulose, or synthetic. The choice of casing affects the sausage's texture and appearance.Stuffing Machines: Industrial sausage stuffers fill the casings uniformly and can be adjusted for different sizes and types of sausages.5. Linking and TyingAfter stuffing, sausages are linked and tied to the desired length.Manual or Automated: This can be done by hand or using automated linking machines that ensure uniform size and shape.6. Smoking and Cooking (for smoked sausages)Many sausages undergo smoking and cooking to enhance flavor, texture, and shelf life.Smoking: Sausages are hung in smoking chambers where they are exposed to smoke from burning wood chips or liquid smoke. This process adds flavor and acts as a preservative.Cooking: The sausages are cooked to a specific internal temperature, ensuring they are safe to eat. This can be done in the smoking chamber or separate steam cookers.7. CoolingAfter smoking and cooking, sausages must be cooled to stop the cooking process and prepare them for packaging.Cooling Methods: Include air cooling in controlled environments or immersion in cold water. Rapid cooling is essential to maintain product quality and safety.8. PackagingThe final step is packaging, which protects the sausages and extends their shelf life.Packaging Materials: Include vacuum packs, modified atmosphere packaging (MAP), or shrink wrapping. These materials prevent contamination and preserve freshness.Packaging Machines: Automated packaging machines are used to package sausages quickly and efficiently, ensuring a tight seal and uniform presentation.Quality Control and SafetyThroughout the sausage production process, rigorous quality control measures are implemented.Hygiene and Sanitation: Strict protocols are followed to prevent contamination. This includes regular cleaning of equipment and facilities, as well as personal hygiene practices for workers.Temperature Control: Maintaining proper temperatures during grinding, mixing, stuffing, and storage is crucial to prevent bacterial growth.Testing: Regular testing for microbial contamination, moisture content, and other quality parameters ensures the sausages meet safety standards and regulatory requirements.Modern Innovations in Sausage ProductionAutomation and Robotics: Enhances efficiency and consistency in grinding, mixing, stuffing, and packaging processes.Advanced Preservation Techniques: Use of high-pressure processing (HPP) and other methods to extend shelf life without compromising quality.Nutritional Enhancement: Incorporation of functional ingredients, such as reduced-fat options, added fibers, or probiotics.Sustainability: Adoption of eco-friendly practices, such as using renewable energy, reducing waste, and utilizing biodegradable packaging materials.ConclusionThe technology of sausage production has evolved significantly, incorporating advanced machinery and strict quality control measures to produce high-quality, safe, and flavorful products. By understanding each stage of the process, from meat selection to packaging, producers can ensure that their sausages meet consumer expectations and regulatory standards. The continuous innovation in this field promises even better products and more efficient production methods in the future.

Requirements for Finished Meat Products

The production of finished meat products, such as sausages, requires adherence to stringent quality and safety standards. These requirements ensure that the products are safe for consumption, have the desired sensory characteristics, and meet regulatory guidelines. This article outlines the key requirements for finished meat products, focusing on quality control, safety standards, and regulatory compliance.1. Quality Control Parametersa. Sensory AttributesAppearance: The product should have a consistent color, shape, and size. For example, sausages should have a uniform appearance without any discoloration or uneven casing.Texture: The texture should be appropriate for the type of meat product. For instance, sausages should have a firm, but not tough, bite.Flavor and Aroma: The product should have the expected taste and smell, free from off-flavors or odors that indicate spoilage or contamination.b. Physical CharacteristicsMoisture Content: The moisture level should be controlled to ensure proper texture and shelf life. Excess moisture can lead to spoilage.Fat Content: Fat content should be within specified limits to ensure flavor and mouthfeel, as well as nutritional labeling accuracy.pH Level: Proper pH levels are crucial for product stability, safety, and texture. The pH affects microbial growth and shelf life.2. Safety Standardsa. Microbiological SafetyPathogen Control: Finished meat products must be free from harmful bacteria, viruses, and parasites such as Salmonella, E. coli, and Listeria. Regular microbiological testing is conducted to ensure compliance.Spoilage Organisms: Control of spoilage organisms like lactic acid bacteria and yeast is essential to maintain product quality and shelf life.b. Chemical SafetyResidue Limits: The product must be free from harmful levels of chemical residues, including pesticides, antibiotics, and hormones. Testing for these substances ensures compliance with regulatory limits.Additives and Preservatives: The use of additives and preservatives should comply with regulations. Commonly used substances like nitrates/nitrites in sausages must be within permissible limits to prevent health risks.Physical SafetyForeign Objects: The product must be free from physical contaminants such as metal fragments, plastic pieces, or bone shards. Metal detectors and X-ray machines are commonly used to detect and remove these contaminants.3. Regulatory Compliancea. Labeling RequirementsNutritional Information: Labels must include accurate nutritional information, including calories, fat, protein, carbohydrates, and sodium content.Ingredients List: All ingredients, including additives and allergens, must be clearly listed on the label.Claims: Any health claims or statements about the product, such as "low fat" or "organic," must be substantiated and comply with regulatory guidelines.b. Packaging StandardsMaterial Safety: Packaging materials must be food-grade and safe for contact with meat products. They should not leach harmful substances into the product.Label Integrity: Labels should be securely attached and resistant to damage during transportation and handling.Traceability: Packaging should include batch numbers, production dates, and other information to ensure traceability in case of recalls.4. Storage and Distribution RequirementsTemperature Control: Finished meat products must be stored and transported at appropriate temperatures to prevent spoilage. For example, refrigerated products should be kept at

0-4°C (32-39°F), while frozen products should be kept at -18°C (0°F) or lower.Shelf Life: The product should have a clearly marked expiration date, and its shelf life must be validated through stability testing.Hygiene Practices: Proper hygiene practices must be followed during storage and distribution to prevent contamination.5. Good Manufacturing Practices (GMP) and Hazard Analysis Critical Control Point (HACCP)GMP Compliance: Adherence to GMP ensures that the products are consistently produced and controlled according to quality standards. This includes sanitation, personnel hygiene, and equipment maintenance.HACCP Plans: Implementing HACCP plans helps identify and control potential hazards in the production process, ensuring food safety from raw material reception to final product distribution.The requirements for finished meat products are comprehensive, covering various aspects of quality, safety, and regulatory compliance. By adhering to these standards, producers can ensure that their products are safe, high-quality, and meet consumer expectations. Continuous monitoring and improvement of production processes are essential to maintaining these standards and staying compliant with evolving regulations.

Assortment of Sausage Products

Sausage products come in a wide variety, each offering unique flavors, textures, and culinary uses. From traditional recipes to modern innovations, the assortment of sausage products caters to diverse tastes and preferences worldwide. This article explores the popular types and varieties of sausage products available:1. Fresh SausagesFresh sausages are typically uncooked and require cooking before consumption. They are known for their juicy texture and vibrant flavors.Italian Sausage: Seasoned with fennel, garlic, and sometimes red pepper flakes, available in mild and hot varieties.bratwurst: Originating from Germany, made with pork, veal, or beef, seasoned with nutmeg, coriander, and white pepper.Chorizo: A Spanish sausage flavored with smoked paprika, garlic, and vinegar, available in sweet and spicy varieties.Breakfast Sausage: Often made with pork and seasoned with sage, thyme, and black pepper, served alongside breakfast dishes.2. Cooked and Smoked SausagesThese sausages are fully cooked during production, often smoked to enhance flavor and shelf life. They can be eaten cold or reheated.Kielbasa: A Polish sausage made with pork or a combination of pork and beef, seasoned with garlic and marjoram, smoked for added flavor.Andouille: A spicy sausage from Cajun cuisine, made with pork, seasoned with garlic, onion, and cayenne pepper, smoked over pecan wood.Smoked Sausage: Generally made with pork, beef, or a combination, smoked to impart a smoky flavor, often used in stews and casseroles.Frankfurters: Also known as hot dogs, made from finely ground meat (usually pork, beef, or a blend), smoked and cured.3. Dry-Cured and Fermented SausagesDry-cured and fermented sausages undergo a curing process, where they are dried and often fermented to develop complex flavors.Salami: A type of Italian dry-cured sausage made with pork, seasoned with garlic, peppercorns, and sometimes wine, aged for weeks to months.Pepperoni: A popular American variety of dry-cured sausage, seasoned with paprika, chili peppers, and garlic, aged for a tangy flavor.Chorizo Seco: A dry-cured Spanish sausage, seasoned similarly to fresh chorizo but cured for several weeks to develop its characteristic flavor.4. Specialty and Regional

Sausages These sausages reflect regional traditions and local ingredients, offering distinctive flavors and culinary uses. Merguez: A North African and Middle Eastern sausage made with lamb or beef, spiced with cumin, coriander, and harissa, often grilled or pan-fried. Boudin Blanc and Boudin Noir: French sausages made with pork or chicken and flavored with spices, with Boudin Blanc being white (no blood) and Boudin Noir being black (with blood). Morcilla: A Spanish blood sausage made with pork blood, rice, onions, and spices, cooked and often served with bread or used in stews. Linguiça: A Portuguese sausage made with pork, garlic, and paprika, often smoked, and used in various Portuguese dishes. 5. Vegetarian and Plant-Based Sausages With the rise of vegetarian and vegan diets, there are now sausage products made entirely from plant-based ingredients. Plant-Based Sausages: Made from ingredients like soy protein, pea protein, or mushrooms, seasoned to mimic traditional sausage flavors. Seitan Sausages: Made from wheat gluten, seasoned and cooked to resemble the texture and taste of meat sausages. Culinary Uses Grilling: Many sausages are ideal for grilling, such as bratwurst, Italian sausage, and merguez.Stews and Casseroles: Sausages like smoked sausage and kielbasa add hearty flavor to stews and casseroles.Appetizers: Sliced and served as appetizers, particularly dry-cured sausages like salami and chorizo.Sandwiches and Wraps: Frankfurters and other cooked sausages are commonly used in sandwiches and wraps.The assortment of sausage products reflects the rich culinary traditions from around the world, offering a variety of flavors, textures, and cooking methods. Whether enjoyed fresh, smoked, dry-cured, or as plant-based alternatives, sausages continue to be a versatile and beloved food item in many cultures. From traditional recipes passed down through generations to innovative new flavors, sausage products cater to diverse tastes and preferences, making them a staple in kitchens and restaurants globally.

Composition of Meat Processing Enterprises

Raw Material SourcingEnterprises source raw materials such as beef, pork, poultry, and occasionally game meats from suppliers, which may include farms, slaughterhouses, and meat wholesalers. The quality and sourcing practices of these raw materials are crucial for the final product quality.Processing FacilitiesMeat processing enterprises operate specialized facilities equipped with machinery and equipment for handling, cutting, grinding, mixing, and packaging meat products. These facilities adhere to strict hygiene and safety standards to ensure product quality and consumer safety.Labor ForceSkilled workers, including butchers, meat cutters, machine operators, food scientists, and quality control inspectors, are essential for the daily operations of meat processing enterprises. These professionals ensure that processing activities meet regulatory requirements and maintain product consistency.Quality Assurance and Safety StandardsMeat processing enterprises implement rigorous quality assurance programs and adhere to food safety regulations (such as HACCP - Hazard Analysis Critical Control Point) to prevent contamination, ensure product traceability, and maintain high standards of hygiene throughout the production process.Types of Meat Processing EnterprisesLarge-scale Meat Processing PlantsDescription: These facilities handle large volumes of meat and produce a wide range of processed products. They often operate on an industrial scale and may serve national or international markets.Products: Includes fresh cuts, ground meat, sausages, cured and smoked meats, ready-to-eat meals, and value-added products like marinated meats or pre-cooked items.Examples: Major meat processing corporations that supply supermarkets, restaurants, and food service providers globally.Small to Medium-sized Meat ProcessorsDescription: These enterprises are smaller in scale compared to large plants but still process significant quantities of meat regionally or locally.Products: Offer a variety of fresh and processed meats tailored to local preferences. They may specialize in specific products such as artisanal sausages, smoked meats, or niche market products.Examples: Family-owned butcher shops, regional meat processors supplying local markets or restaurants.Specialty and Artisanal Meat ProducersDescription: These enterprises focus on producing high-quality, artisanal, and often handcrafted meat products using traditional methods and premium ingredients.Products: Specialty sausages, dry-cured meats (e.g., salami, prosciutto), gourmet cuts, and unique flavor profiles that cater to gourmet markets, specialty stores, and upscale restaurants.Examples: Boutique charcuteries, farm-to-table meat processors, and specialty meat shops emphasizing quality, craftsmanship, and unique flavors.Integrated Meat OperationsDescription: These enterprises oversee all stages of meat production, from raising livestock to processing and packaging meat products. They may integrate farming operations with meat processing facilities to maintain quality control and supply chain efficiency.Products: Includes a range of fresh and processed meats under their own brand labels, often marketed as farm-fresh or sustainable products.Examples: Farms with on-site processing facilities, vertically integrated meat companies ensuring quality from farm to fork.Plant-based Meat AlternativesDescription: Emerging in response to consumer demand for plant-based diets, these enterprises specialize in producing meat alternatives from plant-based ingredients.Products: Plant-based burgers, sausages, nuggets, and ground "meat" products designed to mimic the taste and texture of traditional meat products.Examples: Companies producing Beyond Meat, Impossible Foods, and other plant-based protein brands.Meat processing enterprises play a vital role in the food industry by transforming raw meat into a diverse array of products that cater to global consumer preferences. These enterprises vary in size, scope, and specialization, from large-scale facilities supplying supermarkets and food service chains to artisanal producers crafting specialty meats for niche markets. Understanding the composition and types of meat processing enterprises provides insight into the complexity and diversity of the meat processing sector, which continues to evolve in response to changing consumer trends and technological advancements.

Evaluation of beef quality

Evaluating beef quality involves assessing various factors that collectively determine the meat's tenderness, juiciness, flavor, and overall eating experience. Quality evaluation is crucial for both producers and consumers to ensure satisfaction and consistency in meat products. Here are the key aspects considered when evaluating beef quality:

1. Visual AssessmentMarbling: Intramuscular fat distribution within the meat, visible as white

flecks or streaks. Marbling enhances tenderness, juiciness, and flavor.Color: Bright cherry-red to dark red hues are desirable indicators of freshness and quality. Discoloration or brown spots may suggest aging or improper storage.Fat Color: Creamy white fat indicates good quality, while yellowish or grayish fat may suggest age or diet variations.

2. Sensory AttributesTenderness: Describes the ease of chewing and digestibility. Factors influencing tenderness include muscle location, age at slaughter, and cooking method.Juiciness: Amount of moisture retained in the meat during cooking. Juiciness enhances the eating experience and is influenced by fat content and cooking technique.Flavor: A combination of taste and aroma characteristics. Factors affecting flavor include breed, diet, aging process, and cooking method.Palatability: Overall enjoyment of the meat, combining tenderness, juiciness, and flavor.

3. Grading SystemsUSDA Beef Grading: In the United States, beef is graded based on marbling and maturity. Grades include Prime (highest marbling), Choice, Select, and lower grades.EUROP Grading: Common in Europe,

grades range from E (highest quality) to P (lowest quality) based on conformation (muscle development) and fat covering.Japanese Beef Grading: Wagyu beef is graded on a scale from 1 to 5, with higher numbers indicating superior marbling and quality.

4. Meat CompositionFat Content: Moderate intramuscular fat enhances flavor and tenderness. Excessive external fat may impact consumer preference.Protein Content: Higher protein content generally indicates better nutritional value and may influence cooking characteristics.

5. Production FactorsAnimal Breed: Certain breeds are known for superior meat quality characteristics, such as Wagyu and Angus for marbling.Feeding Regimen: Grass-fed vs. grain-fed diets can influence flavor, color, and fat composition.Age at Slaughter: Younger animals typically yield more tender meat compared to older animals.Handling and Processing: Proper handling and processing practices ensure minimal stress and maintain meat quality post-slaughter.

6. Technological EvaluationInstrumental Methods: Utilizes machines to measure meat characteristics

objectively, such as tenderness (shear force), water-holding capacity, and color (spectrophotometry).Quality Control Checks: Ensures compliance with food safety standards, including microbiological testing for pathogens and chemical residue analysis.

7. Consumer PerceptionConsumer Preferences: Varies based on cultural, regional, and personal preferences for tenderness, flavor intensity, and cooking methods.Packaging and Presentation: Proper packaging preserves freshness and enhances appeal, influencing consumer choice.ConclusionEvaluating beef quality is a multifaceted process involving visual assessment, sensory analysis, grading systems, and consideration of production factors. Each aspect contributes to determining the meat's overall quality, ensuring that consumers receive a satisfying and consistent eating experience. Producers, retailers, and consumers alike benefit from understanding these evaluation criteria to make informed decisions about purchasing and preparing beef products.

Nutritional value of beef

Beef is a nutrient-dense food that provides essential nutrients necessary for overall health and well-being. The nutritional value of beef can vary based on factors such as the cut of meat, cooking method, and animal husbandry practices.

Here's an overview of the key nutrients found in beef and their health benefits:

MacronutrientsProteinBeef is a rich source of high-quality protein, essential for muscle repair, growth, and overall body maintenance.Protein content varies by cut and leaner cuts generally have higher protein-to-fat ratios.FatBeef contains both saturated and unsaturated fats.Saturated Fat: Provides energy and helps maintain cell structure. Leaner cuts of beef have lower saturated fat content.Monounsaturated Fat: Predominantly oleic acid, which is also found in olive oil and has heart-healthy benefits.Polyunsaturated Fat: Includes omega-3 and omega-6 fatty acids, which are important for brain function and reducing inflammation.MicronutrientsVitaminsB Vitamins: Beef is a significant source of B vitamins, including B12, B6, niacin (B3), riboflavin (B2), and thiamine (B1). These vitamins play roles in energy metabolism, red blood cell production, and nerve function. Vitamin D: Important for bone health, immune function, and inflammation regulation. Vitamin E: Acts as an antioxidant, protecting cells from damage caused by free radicals. MineralsIron: Beef is one of the best sources of heme iron, which is more easily absorbed by the body compared to non-heme iron found in plant-based foods. Iron is crucial for oxygen transport in red blood cells and overall energy production. Zinc: Supports immune function, wound healing, and metabolism. Selenium: Acts as an antioxidant and supports thyroid function. Other NutrientsCreatineFound in muscle tissue, creatine supplies energy to muscles during high-intensity exercise and may improve athletic performance. CollagenFound in connective tissue and bone, collagen provides structural support and may benefit joint health and skin elasticity.

Health BenefitsMuscle Maintenance and Growth: Protein in beef supports muscle repair, growth, and maintenance. Iron Absorption: Heme iron in beef is highly bioavailable, helping prevent iron deficiency anemia. Brain and Nerve Function: B vitamins contribute to cognitive function and nervous system health.

Heart Health: Lean cuts of beef can be part of a heart-healthy diet when consumed in moderation and as part of a balanced diet.ConsiderationsLean vs. Fatty Cuts: Choosing lean cuts of beef reduces saturated fat intake while still providing essential nutrients.Cooking Methods: Grilling, broiling, or roasting beef without excessive added fats helps retain its nutritional value.Portion Size: Moderation is key, as excessive consumption of red and processed meats has been associated with increased health risks.ConclusionBeef is a nutrient-rich food that provides essential proteins, fats, vitamins, and minerals necessary for overall health. Including lean cuts of beef in a balanced diet can contribute to meeting daily nutrient requirements and supporting various bodily functions. Understanding the nutritional value of beef helps consumers make informed choices about incorporating it into their diets while considering health and dietary goals.

Technical safety rules in the process of food production

In the process of food production, adhering to technical safety rules is crucial to ensure the production of safe, high-quality food products that meet regulatory standards and consumer expectations. These rules encompass a range of practices and guidelines aimed at preventing contamination, ensuring hygiene, and maintaining product integrity throughout the production process. Here are some key technical safety rules:

1. Facility and Equipment DesignHygienic Design: Facilities and equipment should be designed to facilitate easy cleaning and sanitation, minimizing harborage points for bacteria and other contaminants.Material Compatibility: Use of food-grade materials for equipment and surfaces that come into contact with food to prevent leaching of harmful substances.Separation of Production Areas: Clearly defined zones for raw material handling, processing, packaging, and storage to prevent cross-contamination.

2. Personal Hygiene PracticesHandwashing: Strict protocols for handwashing with soap and water before entering production areas or handling food.Personal Protective Equipment (PPE): Requirement of PPE such as hairnets, gloves, and aprons to prevent contamination from personnel.

3. Cleaning and Sanitation ProceduresCleaning

Protocols: Regular and thorough cleaning of equipment, utensils, and surfaces using approved detergents and sanitizers.Sanitization: Application of sanitizers to kill harmful microorganisms and prevent their growth on surfaces.

4. Pest ControlPreventative Measures: Implementation of pest control measures such as traps, baits, and monitoring to prevent entry and infestation of pests that can contaminate food.Regular Inspections: Scheduled inspections and maintenance of facilities to identify and address potential pest entry points.

5. Temperature ControlRefrigeration: Proper refrigeration and storage temperatures to prevent bacterial growth and spoilage of perishable foods.Cooking and Heating: Ensuring foods reach and maintain appropriate temperatures during cooking and hot holding to destroy pathogens.

6. Allergen ManagementIdentification and Labeling: Clear identification and labeling of allergenic ingredients to prevent cross-contact during production and packaging.Separation: Segregation of allergen-containing ingredients and products to prevent unintended allergen

exposure.

7. Hazard Analysis Critical Control Point (HACCP)Hazard Identification: Systematic assessment of biological, chemical, and physical hazards at each stage of food production.Critical Control Points (CCPs): Establishment of critical control points where preventive measures can be applied to eliminate or minimize identified hazards.

8. Quality Control and TestingProduct Testing: Regular testing for microbial contamination, chemical residues, and other quality parameters to ensure compliance with safety standards.Traceability: Ability to trace raw materials and finished products throughout the production process and supply chain in case of recalls or quality issues.

9. Training and DocumentationEmployee Training: Ongoing training programs for personnel on food safety practices, hygiene, and emergency procedures.Record Keeping: Maintaining accurate records of cleaning schedules, maintenance logs, supplier documentation, and corrective actions taken.

10. Regulatory ComplianceLegal Requirements: Adherence to local, national, and international regulations governing food safety and quality standards.Audits and Inspections: Participation in regulatory audits and inspections to ensure compliance with food safety laws and regulations.Adopting and strictly following technical safety rules in food production is essential for safeguarding public health, maintaining consumer trust, and complying with regulatory requirements. These rules encompass comprehensive measures from facility design to personnel hygiene, cleaning protocols, hazard control, and compliance with quality standards. By implementing robust food safety practices, food producers can mitigate risks, prevent foodborne illnesses, and produce safe and high-quality food products for consumers worldwide.

www.ingramcontent.com/pod-product-compliance
Lightning Source LLC
LaVergne TN
LVHW010218070526
838199LV00062B/4643